SELECTIONS FROM

LES AMOURS JAUNES

Une âme et pas de violon.

"Epitaphe"

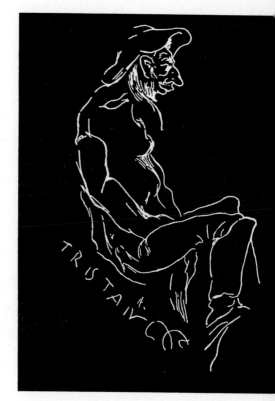

TRISTAN CORBIÈRE
From one of his self-portraits

TRISTAN CORBIÈRE: Selections from

LES AMOURS JAUNES

Translated with an Introduction and Notes

by C. F. MacINTYRE

UNIVERSITY OF CALIFORNIA PRESS
BERKELEY AND LOS ANGELES: 1954

UNIVERSITY OF CALIFORNIA PRESS
BERKELEY AND LOS ANGELES

CAMBRIDGE UNIVERSITY PRESS
LONDON, ENGLAND

COPYRIGHT, 1954, BY
THE REGENTS OF THE UNIVERSITY OF CALIFORNIA

L. C. CATALOG CARD NO. 54–6472

PRINTED IN THE UNITED STATES OF AMERICA
BY THE UNIVERSITY OF CALIFORNIA PRINTING DEPARTMENT

A LA MÉMOIRE DE

SAM FARQUHAR

BON COPAIN

PREFACE

THIS BOOK has required more help and revisions than any other I have done. First, I want to acknowledge the care and time of Mr. Harold A. Small, Editor of the University of California Press. Mr. Small and Professors William Hardy Alexander, Mathurin Dondo, Michel Loève, and Warren Ramsey, of the University, formed a quinquevirate of precision and taste.

Stimulation, encouragement, and admonitions from Enid Starkie of Oxford University, from Georges Connes of the University of Dijon, from Yves-Gérard Le Dantec, who has now edited two presentations of Corbière's poems, from Tristan Tzara, another of Corbière's editors, from Philippe Soupault, the French Surrealist poet, and from Professor Francis Carmody of the University of California, have goaded me and warmed my cockles, monitored and restrained my inadvertencies, and have all united to make this a better and more accurate piece of work.

I want Sam Farquhar's spirit to have this book because it was on New Year's Day, 1936, one of my most Spartan mornings, that we first met and began a relationship which has since resulted in the publication, by the University of California Press, of my Baudelaire, Verlaine, two books of Rilke's poems, and now the Corbière.

Many unnamed Bretons in the poet's towns of Morlaix and Roscoff gave me unwitting assistance, took me to birthplace and grave, showed me keepsakes of the poet, and otherwise bucked me up. Some even had personal reminiscences of Corbière, and I felt a small aureole of glory while talking with the old librarian in Morlaix and an old woman who had known the poet in his youth, maybe a servant, but one who had seen my man. And it is from such contacts, rather than from hours in the Bibliothèque Nationale, that a more human labor comes forth.

C. F. M.

Guadalajara, Mexico
November 1, 1953

CONTENTS

ARMOR

GENS DE MER

RONDELS POUR APRES

x

INTRODUCTION

I

IN THE MOST roundabout, left-handed fashion imaginable it pleases me to approach the strangest and most exciting poet of late nineteenth-century France. Chip on shoulder, thumb at nose he stands, spitting in a gutter, shouting his bastardy—for he is out of some glaucous-haired sea nymph by Villon: a perverse and defiant creature, yet pathetic because the spirit of love in the man had been willfully contorted.

At least three several factors are to be held accountable for the oddities and nuances manifested everywhere in his life and his work: his father was a remarkable man; the boy had ill health, was but sketchily educated and hugely spoiled; and he was a genius. I hope the following translations will help prove the last point. The second is merely a matter of biography which I shall substantiate with the meager material I have been able to find. As for Tristan's father, Edouard Corbière, Rémy de Gourmont said, after a reading of Edouard's novel *Le Négrier*: "The same spirit, with talent and a sharpened nervous system, and you have Tristan."

The future father of the poet was born in 1793, the son of a captain in both the army and the marines: a man of parts, apparently, since some of his verse, with that of a dozen other Breton poets, was published in *Soirées bretonnes* (Bibliothèque de Brest—destroyed in 1943). Edouard was by turns a marine, a midshipman, a polemical journalist, a sea captain, an editor, and a poet and novelist. He helped found a steamship company for traffic between Le Havre and Morlaix, and in 1842 gave up his editorial work and most of his writing and settled in the town which was henceforth to be his home. His wife, Marie-Angélique-Aspasie Puyo, was of a substantial Breton family, and her father left her an estate of almost seignorial proportions, Coatcongar, on the plateau about two miles east

I

of Morlaix. The husband, then past fifty, and the wife of eighteen thus came to live near the place that was also the headquarters of the company of which he was now president.

Edouard's books had made him many friends and he was something of a celebrity in literary circles; he had fought for freedom of the press; eventually he was asked to run for the Chamber of Deputies. He seems, however, to have preferred his repose and solitude; and he was by now almost sixty.

Of the poet's mother we know but little. She devoted herself to her son during his childhood, and when he fell ill at fifteen she was over-solicitous; Tristan is said to have protested: "Don't torment yourself with your duties . . ."

II

Tristan was born, July 16 or 18, 1845, at Coatcongar; his baptismal names, which he later discarded, were Edouard-Joachim. Coatcongar's seventeenth-century house, with its shutters and urns, is most dignified, and the surrounding forest of oaks, lindens, elms, and pines is full of romantic and winding paths, but contains also several classic plantations in long alleys, with vistas. Yet, strangely enough, none of this landscape is used in *Les Amours jaunes;* the sea, the barren beaches, salt marshes, and reefs afford most of the background. The child preferred this to the schoolroom, and early began all sorts of tricks—such as taking drugs to make himself sick—to keep out of school. When he was ten he started reading his father's books, and these had a profound influence on turning him to Brittany and the sea as the sources of many of his best poems, just as the seafaring generations before him must have stimulated his interest in boats.

When he was fifteen a crisis occurred in his disease, which was some form of rheumatism, apparently complicated—at least later—by tuberculosis. His mother took him to Nantes to be under the care of his uncle, Dr. Chenantais (the father of the pseudonymous Pol Kalig, a younger cousin who later helped to get Tristan's book into the hands of Verlaine: an act, simple in itself, which was the beginning of Corbière's fame as a poet).

He seems to have learned some Latin, for he used several Latin tags in his poems. But suddenly his health broke; he grew emaciated and pale, and the rheumatism from which he had suffered in childhood forced him to give up his education in midflight. He still had thirteen years to live, and somehow he managed, even in his capricious and wholly undisciplined way of living, to create the poems which have placed him among the foremost French poets since Baudelaire.

Thus sick, half-educated, with no career planned, this tall, thin youth began his life in Roscoff, where he was soon to make a somewhat malodorous reputation as a blagueur, practical joker, and playboy. Apparently the steamship company was prospering, for his father kept him well supplied with money. At the Pâtisserie Passini, which in those days took the place of an *hôtel-pension,* he made a lifelong friend of the host, Le Gad, and used to amuse the clientèle by drawing caricatures, probably on the tablecloth. I imagine he loved the local shellfish, the fabulous vegetables produced by the mild climate, and *crêpes bretonnes,* thin pancakes about a foot in diameter, sprinkled with sugar; and certainly he liked to drink.

About this time he began to wear an odd costume, a mixture of galley slave's hat, sea boots, short-sleeved shirt; he let his beard grow untrimmed; and he acquired Tristan II, a dog which Le Goffic says was "the most wretched water spaniel in all Armorica." Tristan had taken his alias from a hero of legend, Tristan of Lyonesse, whom he thought of in an almost fraternal way. As for the man and the dog, they were inseparable, and were "still remembered in Roscoff" when Le Goffic wrote about them, a lifetime later. A municipal edict required that all dogs be led on leash; so next day the dog appeared at one end of a block-long tether, while the master, at the other end, was peacefully seated outside the café, enjoying the havoc the rope made among pedestrians. The ordinance, alas, did not limit the length of the cord. "These eccentricities, and others less innocent," continues his biographer, "rapidly made the young man a local celebrity."

He had a sailboat, small enough to be hauled at night into his living quarters and used as a bed. Presumably, by day the young man and the dog went sailing, and at night Tristan I slept in his kelp-perfumed boat-bed, with Tristan II curled up alongside in a fish basket as if in a trailed dinghy. Buoyed in this piscatorial aroma, how the spaniel must have tossed in mad thalassic dreams during which he pursued marvelous catfish and yapped challengingly at dogfish, barking away undersea with muffled silver bubbles of silent ferocity, beautiful elongated ciphers of air which rose slowly to the surface and burst with long-delayed detonations.

Anyone ought to enjoy Tristan's amusements at the expense of the Roscoff bourgeoisie. A fad had struck the Faithful; they believed that the end of the world was at hand. So Le Gad and the poet borrowed and rented a great number of muskets, blunderbusses, and pistols, which they fired off in a terrible fusillade when the good people began to sing. The whole congregation ran terror-stricken out of the church; and they probably never forgave Tristan, who gravely saluted them and assured them he had meant no harm. Quite of a piece with this story is another: after he had been in Italy, he suddenly appeared one afternoon on the balcony of his father's house in Morlaix dressed as a bishop and dispensed benign episcopal blessings on all who passed. Of course, substantial citizens couldn't understand why the son of an eminent man of the town should behave so.

Tristan deliberately wrecked a small sailboat on the rocks, so that his father "would give him another, a larger one." This is the trick of a spoiled brat. In fact, the boat was replaced by the cutter *Le Négrier,* in which the young man took all sorts of chances in any kind of weather. When the barometer dropped and the storm signal was hoisted to warn fishermen, the young poet would push off his craft for a little cruise. The old sailors thought he was possessed of the devil, and his thin figure gave them good reason to call him an *Ankou* (Breton for Death). Thus it is easy to see why he became almost a legend within his lifetime.

The neighbors on the Quai de Léon heard sometimes a hurdy-gurdy being ground by the sad poet, or sometimes it was a violin, which he played, it is said, with a fair degree of talent. This is probably the real Tristan, without the mask of bravado. There is a story that one day he was at the house of his aunt, a woman who seems to have understood him, his tenderness, and his need of love. Suddenly, he departed brusquely, and an hour later returned with the bloody heart of a sheep he had got from the butcher. "Look," he said, "here is my heart." (Rousselot maintains that the recipient was a prostitute in Morlaix. *A chacun son goût*.) All adolescents suffer, although most people forget it when they get older; Tristan was supersensitive, he was in ill health, without any definite pursuit, and he felt that he was very ugly. His photographs do not show a monster, but all his self-portraits are hideously exaggerated. (See, for example, the one facing the title page of this book.) In the poem "Guitare" he exclaims, "Je suis si laid!" And in a poem which I do not translate he likens himself to a toad.

In Roscoff there was the usual café group of minor artists, most of whom did not become famous afterward. The conversations must have been exciting to the young sailor who was already beginning to write poetry, although his kind of poetry had little in common— nothing at all, in fact—with the usual sort of stuff read aloud in small groups. Tristan was picking up his material in the course of walks around the wharves, lending a hand with a throw-line, admiring the morning's catch, drinking hot grogs on cold foggy mornings in smoky bistros where the fishermen and sailors hung out, and swapping yarns of his own imagining for the perhaps no more true tales of the sailors, retired smugglers, and ex-privateersmen. And at night they probably sang bawdy chanteys to which the spaniel must have added an earnest tenor. All this is merely conjecture, but I am convinced it is the stuff of which Tristan was thinking, milling over in verses as rough as the Channel waves while he was making a long tack, with knee hooked over the tiller, and smoking his pipe on a warm, sunny day with a fair wind.

By 1870, says Martineau (*Tristan Corbière,* p. 57), almost all the poems of ARMOR, GENS DE MER, and RACCROCS had been written. But he had already said (pp. 53–54): "The dates [Corbière] has put at the end of many of the poems . . . are untrustworthy, often merely fantastic." It doesn't make much difference, so long as the poet finally got his book written; not a few poets have put their first

5

achievements last. Perhaps he realized that in Brittany and the sea he had more abiding matter for his devotion than in the woman he was soon to meet who was the inspiration for the first three parts of *Les Amours jaunes.*

Tristan was twenty-six when, in 1871, the unexpected event occurred which was to upset his life and give him the title for another part of his book in which is revealed a hitherto nonexistent or unpredicted personality: Tristan as lover and cynical *Weltmensch.*

III

Count Rodolphe Battine, heir to an estate near Mans, and recently an officer in the Franco-Prussian War, in which he had been wounded, came to Roscoff to complete his convalescence. He was a "distinguished person" (I suppose Martineau means that the Count dressed well and had an air—certainly Rodolphe had no other pretensions); he spent money freely, and gambled unsuccessfully. As is to be expected, when a hero is convalescing he needs distraction: the Count had thoughtfully brought his with him. Armida-Josefina Cuchiani, an Italienne as her name implies, was an actress when the Count picked her up in the wings of some small theater—as Baudelaire had met the fatal Jeanne. "She was tall and strongly made, with expressive blue eyes, and she had thick blonde hair. In Paris she was not one of those women who impel the passer-by to turn round and gaze; but in Roscoff she dazzled!" (Martineau, p. 58.)

The first evening at dinner in the hotel, Tristan drew their caricatures and established relations. Next morning, he attacked at breakfast; an excursion was planned, and from then on there were daily sailing trips, little walks, et cetera. The impact of la Cuchiana must have been terrific on the poet, who seems before this to have shown but little interest in women, at least in his poems. Certainly we have here the beginning of the series including "A une camarade" and the other misogynistic embittered verses against, not women, but a woman, in LES AMOURS JAUNES, the title section.

Biographers insist that she loved the poet, but that her conduct, before and after this liaison, showed her to be without scruple. She had the grand manner in public and "dissimulated the worst turpi-

6

tudes," says Martineau. The Count seems to have been singularly complacent about the little triangle. He was blasé, probably bored with the lack of gay life in the small town; he was perhaps cooling toward his mistress (although he later made her his heir), and he was undoubtedly amused by the poet's vivacity and originality and by the cruises taken on Tristan's new boat—for the young lover had immediately bought a larger and more comfortable vessel. On one of these trips, Corbière gave the actress the name "Marcelle." The reader must get what he can from these poems themselves; whether the poet had grounds for his vituperations, or whether he was using the situation as a stimulant, is an unanswerable question. (I must be allowed a word of protest here: whatever may have been the relationship between them, certainly no woman could be expected to feel very coöperative if she read in manuscript any of the "love" poems in LES AMOURS JAUNES.)

At the end of six months, the Count returned to Paris, taking Marcelle dutifully in tow, and Tristan was left with his memories. The poet in him probably got more work done then than at any other time. We owe "Le Poète contumace" to this lonely post-mortem period.

Whether or not the girl ever saw this poem, she apparently had no intention of playing Yseult to this already dying lover. Consequently, early in 1872, he went down to Paris. A friend found him a top-floor studio in one of those quaint enclosed courts in Montmartre which are called *cités*. This one was the Cité Gaillard, at the top of the Rue Blanche.

Corbière, however, did no painting in his studio. Perhaps the impact of all the pictures in the Louvre, the Luxembourg, the Jeu de Paume, and so on, had overcome him. To one of his friends, who liked to paint sheep, he said: "You paint them worse than Jacques, who painted them worse than Troyon, who painted them worse than nature." This is a sample of his somewhat involved conversational method.

During this time, Tristan kept busy making miniature boats which he prepared with great care and "exquisite art" and then destroyed by stepping on them. He also made for one of his friends a chandelier which consisted of two swords crossed through a large potato and furnished with tapers. He assisted at another party disguised as a beggar and singing Breton songs.

He wasted no time in the literary cafés, which even then were affected by those who prefer talking to doing. Most of his evenings were spent with the Count and Marcelle. The Count got him finally to a first-class tailor, and for a while Corbière seems to have gone about the night life of the city quite *comme il faut,* in an elegant dress suit and with a top hat. (To what depths will a man not stoop in his efforts to please a woman!) But naturally, so distinguished a person as the Count could not be seen about town with a Tristan in his Breton sailor costume.

To his great joy, the pair decided once to make a hasty return trip to the north coast. "The poet stood his sea boots upright and threw socks, handkerchiefs, and flasks of perfume" into them. These were his trunks for the trip. (Martineau, p. 73.) Among other eccentricities, he made a self-portrait with a big toad sitting on his chest; and over the mantel he nailed a dried flattened real toad, for verification. For a while he attempted, without success, to sell some of his drawings to the periodicals. Finally he returned to literature as a medium.

For a long time he had hoped to publish "Gens de mer," and had even composed a preface; several of his poems had appeared in *La Vie parisienne,* in six issues in 1873. Then finally he met the Glady brothers, who decided to publish the book after Tristan should have added a substantial number of other poems and a self-portrait—to all of which he objected strenuously but futilely. His father paid for the printing, and an edition of 490 copies was run off in 1873.

The book fell on a deaf public. With customary aplomb, however, the author paid no attention to its apparent failure. Maybe he was having his hands full with Marcelle. "Ces dames sont le remède," he had assured an unfledged young poet in "A un Juvénal de lait." The book was dedicated, quite properly, À L'AUTEUR DU NÉGRIER. But it was bound, so to speak, between the two parts of a diptych: poems addressed to Marcelle. This has confused several critics, who gallantly want to think that hers is the whole book. The author, however, was too much impressed by his father's accomplishments to have allowed a mere broad, however charming he may have found her, to usurp the old gentleman's place.

At this time the Parnassians, under the tutelage of Leconte de Lisle, had captured those French minds which were open to poetry. Naturally, such a public could not get excited over the unexpected rhymes and rhythms, the individualistic treatment, and the almost foreign subject matter of most of the poems in *Les Amours jaunes.* Bravely enough, however, Corbière began a proposed second volume, to be called "Mirlitons," but produced only five poems for it.

Meanwhile, the Count's father died, and the trio made a hasty visit to the ancestral castle, where Tristan's thin silhouette left the inhabitants stupefied. On their return to Paris, Tristan became gravely ill. He was taken to a hospital, and Marcelle visited him for the last time. He wrote to his parents: "I am at Dubois's, where they make coffins." A cheerful way to announce the inevitable to his family!—but quite typical.

His mother came and took him sadly to Morlaix, where he died March 1, 1875. On his last day he had his room filled with the native heather. He was buried in the family vault in the Saint-Martin cemetery; and his father followed him a few months later.

I have been greatly surprised and saddened to find no record of Tristan's actual grave in the cemetery, or in the records of the period. One vault has simply the family name; a second bears the combined name Vacher-Corbière because at least one collateral seems to have been aware of the local glory of the name and to have added his wife's to his own. Aside from a handful of enthusiasts, librarians, booksellers, local scholars, writers, and painters, who in 1945 held a centennial "Conférence" honoring his memory, his townsmen have been untouched by his fame. The local family even today, I know for a fact, is ashamed of Tristan's unconventional habits and looks on him as a black sheep. I found him well remembered in only four homes in Morlaix and Roscoff. Aside, however, from an unreproducible photograph, a dark and badly painted picture of the spaniel by the poet, a plate and a family clock, a photograph of one of the series of boats, and a copy of a letter, I got no tangible results from two sojourns in Brittany.

9

So few people read poetry! Even in Paris, where there is perhaps more enthusiasm for it than elsewhere in the world, *Les Amours jaunes* fell into Limbo. And there it lay for several years. Then, and this is a moot point, Paterne Berrichon (who seems to have been exceedingly astute about rescuing the fame of dead poets: he was Rimbaud's brother-in-law, and did him an equal service) discovered the book. And someone (several, including Charles Morice and Pol Kalig, claim the honor) made the book known to Verlaine. Morice (*Tristan Corbière,* pp. 22–25) is eloquent about the part he himself played: "It was a winter's night in 1883, when Trézenik and I, turn and turn about, read the precious volume, from cover to cover, to the master of *Sagesse*."

Le Goffic writes (in his preface to the edition of 1926, p. iv): "Verlaine read it, caught fire, and wrote at one sitting the famous study which opens his series of critical essays in *Poètes maudits*." Verlaine sees Corbière as "preëminently a man of scorn, *aes triplex*. His verse is alive, it laughs, weeps a little, mocks itself cleverly, and commits hoaxes and blagues still better." Verlaine also indicated several poems he particularly liked, and made judgments which have influenced my choice of poems to translate.

Actually, it was Huysmans who first drew my attention to Corbière, in his *A rebours*. I must here pay him a belated tribute. It was the ducal nod of his Des Esseintes which forced me to translate a book of the poems of Baudelaire, one of Verlaine, the present book, and another (in manuscript) of the complete poems of Mallarmé. Des Esseintes's monologue in his library adequately sums up the Breton's work so far as a contemporary could see its value. "It was," wrote Huysmans—who had just quoted from the poem entitled "Ça?"—"barely French. The author was talking pidgin, writing his poems as if they were telegrams, suppressing too many verbs, affecting a mocking tone, indulging in the jibes of a low bagman; then, all at once, out of this jumble would squirm curious conceits, dubious affectations, and suddenly a cry of acute pain would start, like a violincello string's breaking. With all that, in this harsh, dry style, wantonly stripped bare, bristling with unusual vocables and unexpected neologisms, flashed many a real 'find' in phrasing, many a stray verse rhymeless yet superb."

Rémy de Gourmont, in one of those too slight essays of his in *Livre des masques,* gives a concise appraisal, prefaced by a statement from one of Corbière's disciples. At the time of Gourmont's essay the notes by Jules Laforgue had not been published in book form; but they have been since, and we shall come to them later. Gourmont then continues, on his own: "All his life, Corbière was ruled and guided by the demon of contradiction. . . . He supposed that one should distinguish oneself from the mass of men by thoughts and actions exactly contrary to theirs; his originality results from the sheer will to be different . . . This is the very *dandysme* of Baudelaire. . . . He has the wit of the bistros and cafés of Montmartre, and of the fo'c'sle. His gifts are formed of the spirit of bravado, baroque, partial to hoaxes, with a gamin's impudence and bad taste, with flashes of genius. He acts like a drunken man, but he is only laboriously awkward; weaving crazy chaplets, patiently making mosaics in which rough little stones from the seacoast crop forth nakedly, . . . because he really loved the sea, and because, despite himself and the madness for paradox, he gives way once in a while to a real intoxication with beauty and true poetry. . . . His verses are often admirable but ambiguous. . . . Like Laforgue, a bit his disciple, he is one of those indubitable but unclassifiable talents, a strange and precious singularity."

Now let Laforgue speak for himself; in *Entretiens Politiques et Littéraires* (July, 1891) appears his essay on Corbière. There he has given these precise definitions: "Bohemian of the Ocean—picaro and vagabond, brusque, succinct, forcing his verses along with a whip . . . strident and shrill as the cries of the seagulls, and tireless as they—without an aesthetic—with nothing at all of poetry or versification, scarcely anything of literature, about them . . . there isn't another verse artist who has so completely freed himself from poetic language. . . . The effect is of a whiplash, the drypoint burin; he is frisky, makes puns and words with rude romantic abruptness—he wants to remain outside of definition, not to be catalogued, to be neither loved nor hated—in short, he wants to be . . . beyond every custom on this or the other side of the Pyrenees." And in *Mélanges posthumes* (pp. 118–128) Laforgue writes (here are some excerpts): "This isn't the originality of someone breaking free from the Romantics and the Parnassians, in that order, but real devil-may-care originality. . . . His art has nothing to do with the poetry of sunsets, of the sky, or the sea [as mere landscape]. . . . He writes like a pirate on the prowl."

But the author of the *Complaintes* was too quick in denying *métier* to Corbière, to whom he owed more than he would admit. Léo Trézenik took him up on it: "Where Corbière has enaureoled himself with a light mist, in the swirls of which the initiates can find themselves, M. Laforgue delights in sitting down in a bottle of ink of the most undeniable opacity."

Léon Durocher, in the thin pamphlet which records his speech at Morlaix when the monument with its sculptured profiles of the two literary Corbières by Bourdelle was presented to the city, includes a reminiscent poem of the days when he had met Tristan in the Chat Noir and they had read the future book together; then the really fine stanza:

> Ton frère, Villon, détaché
> D'un cadre roux, sur tes poèmes
> Et sur mon épaule penché
> M'expliquait tes rimes bohèmes.

> (Your brother Villon, come to life
> out of a painting's red-brown frame,
> leaned on my shoulder, over the poems,
> and explained to me your careless rhymes.)

Prior to this, there had been a "Conférence" to consider the matter and to receive recommendations that the project be carried out. Charles Morice delivered a paper before it (May 28, 1912), which I shall summarize briefly. Corbière's irony, he says, is a product of sadness and pride. There are two types of irony: the affirmative and the negative. "The first proceeds from love and its laughter which can rail implacably at reprobates and liars and give this raillery the inflection of kisses. This is the laugh of Apollo while with an expert hand he flayed the unfortunate Marsyas, that antique patron of parodists—and the laughter of Apollo is also that of Heine and Villiers de l'Isle-Adam. Negative irony is a grimace of impotence. Incapable of supporting a powerful thought, of measuring a heroic gesture, this irony turns them into derision. It is not human, and it has a mechanical grin in its forced gaiety. It detests nature, and is the pestilential product of the boulevard." Corbière's irony, however, is the product—Morice continues—of his great love (as shown, I take it, in his pity and sympathy with the poor wretches in "Le Pardon de Sainte-Anne," "Le Bossu Bitor," and various other poems—though Morice does not help one much here); this love is affirmative and has nothing sickly or negative about it. But it is the poet's incapacity for making a positive affirmation that tortures both his soul and his art. Thus in his frustrations as exhibited in many of the poems of the first four sections of the book—his difficulties with women as typified in Marcelle and his disillusionment about his work—he uses defensively all sorts of puns, irritating accents of bitterness, and the like. Tristan was also in violent reaction to the reigning Parnassian school, for his dreamy and mystic nature was antipathetic to the chilly objectivity and the polished form of the disciples of Leconte de Lisle; but it is when he comes to the "Pardon" and the poems of the sea and its people that Tristan is truly himself and achieves real grandeur.

This is the gist of Morice's short paper. And he praises in particular "La Fin." "When instinct and the love of *plastique* reality open on the world the eyes of a natural idealist, one can predict a great work." Thus it was that Brittany and the sea opened the eyes of Corbière and work of abiding importance was done.

In *Les Destinées mauvaises* (1923), Léon Bocquet (p. 77) puts the author of the first half of the book on equal terms with the poet of the later sections, and he insists on the great novelty of the Parisian poems, and of the Rondels. This is "a new state of poetic sensibility, a spine-tingling sensation hitherto unknown by which is revealed already that mysterious emotion which comes from the most distant dreams, from the misty and as yet undefined background of the spirit. The honor of this discovery has been accorded to Verlaine and the Symbolists, but is it not Corbière who was the originator of this poetry? . . ." (P. 103:) "He is not an artist like any other. Of the poet's trade he had an absolutely personal concept which drove him to seek his themes outside of the easy and the known and then to realize these subjects with full and conscious horror of the familiar and banal. . . . But this poetry is neither so spontaneous nor so negligent as some suppose. He worked scrupulously and patiently over his poems, like a good craftsman."

In the little "Librairie celtique" edition of the poems, 1947, Alexandre Arnoux contributes nothing new to the biography, except that he thinks the Marcelle of the poems was a figment of the poet's imagination which he invented and played with as a whipping-boy for his amusement. He points out (pp. 30–32) that three very dynamic poetic anarchists were born within a decade of one another: Corbière, 1845; Lautréamont, whose *Maldoror* is astonishing stuff, in 1846; and Rimbaud, a sullen prodigy who never allowed himself to finish his work, in 1854. He comments on the fury of their poetic afflatus, their rebellion, their detachment from traditional forms, their anarchic comicality, lucidity, and cruelty, which seem to announce the subversions, the catastrophes, and the terrors of modern life. Rimbaud called it "le temps des assassins."

Tristan Tzara, one of the latest of Corbière's critics, writes, in his preface of 1950: "In *Les Amours jaunes* the will to expression . . . attains a kind of verbal exasperation which, far from being disorder, is on the contrary the coherent development of poetic thought."

André Breton, in his *Anthologie de l'humour noir*, 1950, insists on the defensive character of Corbière's humor. It has no desire to be "funny," but is called into play by the contrast between Tristan's physical uncomeliness and his extraordinary endowment of sensibilities. Rousselot stresses the point: to be young and a Breton, and at the same time to be sickly and weak, where the life of the sea is for the strong, and the sailors' women too are for the strong!—an atrocious verdict, against which Tristan revolted. However it may have been, he derived from it a supplementary power—an exasperation of the spirit of revolt, a wincing of the will to live, which manifest themselves in counter-offensive attack.

14

He was the first, says Breton (pp. 163–164), to "let himself be carried along by the wave of words"; and thus he might be considered a precursor of those more recent French poets who have attempted "automatic writing." Rousselot (pp. 77–78) sharply denies any such thing. Posing as "artiste sans art, à l'envers," Tristan "possessed an art all his own, solid, supple, and perfectly efficient," and "only its novelty and daring have given credence" to the legend.

Rousselot further cites as influences Hugo, Baudelaire, Gavarni, and Daumier. I would add: certain tricks, alas, from Musset; some hints from Gautier; much from Edouard Corbière's material; and finally, certain suggestions from a book of sea poems by Gabriel de La Landelle, *Le Gaillard d'avant: chansons maritimes* (Paris, Dentu, 1862), which was brought to the attention of a "Conférence" held at Morlaix in September, 1947, by Jean de Trigon, who owns the family papers. La Landelle, a former naval officer, was a prolific writer of sea tales and sketches which enjoyed an equal popularity with those of Corbière *père*. I made two efforts to get in touch with M. de Trigon, but he was always traveling elsewhere. The old librarian at Morlaix, who in his youth had seen Tristan, was past ninety, almost blind, and was unable to give me any information. The shelves lay deep in dust, and there was no catalogue.

v

May I add here a brief word about a neglected matter? Corbière's use, abuse, of punctuation is both arbitrary and unhelpful; he dabs in as many dots and dashes as an intoxicated telegraph operator; and perhaps his various printers have joined in the game. Many of these marks I have reproduced in the translations because I could not honestly decide what he intended. When a poem is a dialogue, the difficulty is sometimes insurmountable; a reader simply cannot tell who says what or to whom. When Corbière overpunctuates, he is abstruse; when he does not punctuate at all, he is the fountain-head of the moderns—from Mallarmé and Stefan George to the minor scribblers.

Another point: Corbière sometimes acknowledges the loan of a word, phrase, or line from another poet by underscoring what he borrows, and his printers, as is customary, then use italic type; the French are in sad need of more quotation marks, both single and double. But sometimes he doesn't accord it such acknowledgment. Of course, he expects the well-read Frenchman to spot his obvious unlabeled borrowings, just as we expect mention of a "forest primeval" to be taken in stride, without quotes; yet he is not hesitant about compounding a pastiche without warning if it suits his purpose to do so. Whatever he may take from his predecessors is nevertheless rightly his, as a son takes the nose of his father. Let us leave it at that.

I have arbitrarily taken two poems from the "Appendice" and placed them after "Ça?" For a while these poems, which were first published only in 1890, were forgotten; then Rémy de Gourmont reprinted them in his essay and complained about their absence from the then current edition. They rightly belong before the sonnet series called "Paris." They represent the impact of the great city on the young sailor, a man accustomed to the broad sweep of ocean, the naked brown flanks of the ever-shifting dunes, the craggy coast, the Breton villages with their huddled-down stone houses which, like the very rocks, defy the sea winds and the storms. Naturally he is somewhat lost and at first tries to liken the night sounds of Paris to something familiar: the snarlings of the surf and the scratching of nocturnal crabs along the shingle. He hears the intense, febrile, mosquito-like voice of a city that never sleeps—the pounding roar of day has been muted. The second piece is more bitter and personal; he may be thinking rather of the fate of the artist in a metropolis than of the persons whom he seems to be describing. He means: here, we get what they're willing to dish out to us, and brother, it's damn little!

I have stood beside his nameless tomb, which is in the family plot at Morlaix. But he should have been buried near Roscoff; and it is to a particular beach under the northernmost-jutting promontory there that I propose transporting his spirit for my valediction.

There he sleeps the long sleep to a low berceuse *en Nord-ouest mineur,* within easy reach of the shingle on which his first boat is shored. He sleeps with the ever-faithful Tristan II near by in a shallow grave lined with a fish basket; shallow, I say, because when his quixotic master takes a sudden nocturnal whim to go sailing head-on into those blessèd eternal storms of La Manche, the dog will have to scratch less dirt to free himself and be ready to hop aboard.

⋄   ⋄   ⋄

And now away they tack through the brine-lipped spoondrift,
with sheet and tiller tugging in the skipper's hands,
with bows that spank obsidian waves of night, . . . and maybe
when a ghostly moonlight trickles through the cloud-scuds,
from the deadman's ribs of the Flying Dutchman's prow,
from the poop of Drake's proud galleon, bloodhound after doubloons,
the washed deck of some worm-gnawed blue-jowled Phoenician galley
laden to the gunn'ls with bars of tin from Cornwall,
or from some walrus-mustached Viking's lean wave-walker,
through the mist they'll hear a far-off, thin "Ahoy!"
Then, while silver-footed sea nymphs toll a knell,
faintly answer spaniel-yappings from a salt-drenched cockpit.

ÇA

ÇA?

What?......
(*Shakespeare*)

Des essais? — Allons donc, je n'ai pas essayé!
Etude? — Fainéant, je n'ai jamais pillé.
Volume? — Trop broché pour être relié...
De la copie? — Hélas non, ce n'est pas payé!

Un poème? — Merci, mais j'ai lavé ma lyre.
Un livre? — ... Un livre, encore, est une chose à lire!...
Des papiers? — Non, non, Dieu merci, c'est cousu!
Album? — Ce n'est pas blanc, et c'est trop décousu.

Bouts-rimés? — Par quel bout?... Et ce n'est pas joli!
Un ouvrage? — Ce n'est poli ni repoli.
Chansons? — Je voudrais bien, ô ma petite Muse!...
Passe-temps? — Vous croyez, alors, que ça m'amuse?

— Vers?... vous avez flué des vers?... — Non, c'est heurté.
— Ah, vous avez couru l'Originalité?...
— Non... c'est une drôlesse assez drôle, — *de rue* —
Qui court encor, sitôt qu'elle se sent courue.

— Du *chic* pur? — Eh, qui me donnera des ficelles?
— Du haut vol? Du haut mal? — Pas de râle, ni d'ailes!
— Chose à mettre à la porte? — ... Ou dans une maison
De tolérance. — Ou bien de correction? — Mais non!

— Bon, ce n'est pas classique? — A peine est-ce français!
— Amateur? — Ai-je l'air d'un monsieur à succès?
— Est-ce vieux? — Ça n'a pas quarante ans de service...
— Est-ce jeune? — Avec l'âge, on guérit de ce vice.

OH! THAT?

What? . . .

(Shakespeare)

Essays?—Nonsense, I have not essayed!
A study?—I'm lazy, I've never pilfered around.
A volume?—Too brochure-like to be bound . . .
Copy?—For that, alas, you don't get paid!

A poem?—Thanks, but I have hocked my lyre.
A book?— . . . A book, that's something to be read! . . .
Loose sheets?—No, thank God, it's tight-sewn and entire!
Album?—Not blank, but it lacks a coherent thread.

Rhymed ends?—By which end? . . . And it's little use!
An opus?—It's not polished and polished again.
Songs?—I'd just love that, my little Muse! . . .
Pastime?—You think it's mere amusement, then?

Verses? . . . a flux of verse? . . . —No, it's jerky, see.
—Ah, you've been chasing Originality? . . .
—No . . . she's an odd hussy,—*from the streets*—it's
odd, when you proposition her, she beats it.

Is it pure *chic?*—And who'd teach me that game?
—Does it soar? Or sink convulsed?—Neither flight nor fall!
—A thing for the ashcan?— . . . Or for a house of ill fame.
—The reformatory, even?—Not at all!

—Good, it's not classic?—It is barely French!
—Amateur?—Do I suggest success?
—Old-fashioned?—Well, not forty years off the bench . . .
—New style?—With years, one remedies that vice.

... *ÇA* c'est naïvement une impudente *pose;*
C'est, ou ce n'est pas *ça:* rien ou quelque chose.
— Un chef-d'œuvre? — Il se peut, je n'en ai jamais fait.
— Mais, est-ce du huron, du Gagne, ou du Musset?

— C'est du... mais j'ai mis là mon humble nom d'auteur,
Et mon enfant n'a pas même un titre menteur.
C'est un coup de raccroc, juste ou faux, par hasard...
L'Art ne me connaît pas. Je ne connais pas l'Art.

Préfecture de police, 20 mai 1873.

. . . *THAT* is naïvely just an impudent *pose;*
it is or it isn't *that:* all or nothing, say.
—A masterpiece?—Maybe; I've never made one of those.
—Is it in the style of the Hurons, of Gagne, or Musset?

—It's like . . . I've signed my humble *nom d'auteur,*
and my child has no title that's a lie.
It may be right, or wrong: a hit-or-miss try . . .
Art has never met me. And I don't know Her.

Central police station, May 20, 1873.

PARIS NOCTURNE

> Ce'n'est pas une ville, c'est un monde.

C'est la mer, — calme plat. — Et la grande marée
Avec un grondement lointain s'est retirée...
Le flot va revenir se roulant dans son bruit.
Entendez-vous gratter les crabes de la nuit?

C'est le Styx asséché: le chiffonnier Diogène,
La lanterne à la main, s'en vient avec sans-gêne.
Le long du ruisseau noir, les poètes pervers
Pêchent: leur crâne creux leur sert de boîte à vers.

C'est le champ: pour glaner les impures charpies
S'abat le vol tournant des hideuses harpies;
Le lapin de gouttière à l'affût des rongeurs
Fuit les fils de Bondy, nocturnes vendangeurs.

C'est la mort: la police gît. — En haut l'amour
Fait sa sieste, en têtant la viande d'un bras lourd
Où le baiser éteint laisse sa plaque rouge.
L'heure est seule. Ecoutez: pas un rêve ne bouge.

C'est la vie: écoutez, la source vive chante
L'éternelle chanson sur la tête gluante
D'un dieu marin tirant ses membres nus et verts
Sur le lit de la Morgue... et les yeux grands ouverts.

PARIS BY NIGHT

It's not a city, it's a world.

It's the sea,—dead calm.—And the spring's great tide,
snarling distantly now, has retreated wide . . .
Rumbling, it will roll in from the ebb.
Do you hear the scratching of nocturnal crabs?

It's the dried Styx: here comes Diogenes,
ragpicker, with lantern, wandering at his ease.
The perverse poets by the somber river,
with their hollow skulls for bait-cans, fish forever.

It's the fields: in wheeling flight the hideous hags,
harpies, swoop to glean the dirty rags;
the gutter-rabbit, alert for rats, takes flight
from Bondy's boys, the vintagers of night.

It's death: the cop's laid out.—In an upper room
at rest, love sucks the flesh of a heavy arm
where the slaked kisses leave their rouge in smudges.
The hour's alone. Listen: not a dream budges.

It's life: listen, the living waters shed
the eternal song upon the slimy head
of a sea-god with green naked limbs who lies
on a bed in the Morgue . . . with great wide-open eyes.

PARIS DIURNE

Vois aux cieux le grand rond de cuivre rouge luire,
Immense casserole où le bon Dieu fait cuire
La manne, l'arlequin, l'éternel plat du jour:
C'est trempé de sueur et c'est poivré d'amour.

Les laridons en cercle attendent près du four,
On entend vaguement la chair rance bruire,
Et les soiffards aussi sont là, tendant leur buire;
Le marmiteux grelotte en attendant son tour.

Tu crois que le soleil frit donc pour tout le monde
Ces gras graillons grouillants qu'un torrent d'or inonde?
Non, le bouillon de chien tombe sur nous du ciel.

Eux sont sous le rayon et nous sous la gouttière.
A nous le pot au noir qui froidit sans lumière.
Ma foi, j'aime autant ça que d'être dans le miel!

PARIS BY DAY

Look at the great red copper disk above,
glowing where God heats up in his casserole
manna, scraps, the eternal daily dole:
it's simmering in sweat and peppered with love.

In the vague sizzle of rancid meat that burns,
the scullions squat in a circle round the oven.
The drunks are there, too, holding out their flagons;
a poor wretch has the shakes as he waits his turn.

You think it's for all and sundry the sun fries
those seething gobs of fat in golden grease?
No, on us drips dog-soup from the skies.

Some have sunshine; we live under the eaves.
For us the kettle that's black, no longer hot.
Bah! I'd as lief have that as the honey-pot!

PARIS

(i)

Bâtard de Créole et Breton,
Il vint aussi là — fourmilière,
Bazar où rien n'est en pierre,
Où le soleil manque de ton.

— Courage! On fait queue... Un planton
Vous pousse à la chaîne — derrière! —
... Incendie éteint, sans lumière;
Des seaux passent, vides ou non. —

Là, sa pauvre Muse pucelle
Fit le trottoir en *demoiselle*.
Ils disaient: Qu'est-ce qu'elle vend?

— Rien. — Elle restait là, stupide,
N'entendant pas sonner le vide
Et regardant passer le vent...

PARIS

(i)

Bastard Breton-Créole,
he too to this anthill comes—
this bazaar, not of stone at all,
where there's no style to the sun.

—Hang on! The line's forming . . . A guard—
Keep back of that rope!—shoves you hard.
. . . No light now. The fire is out;
yet buckets pass, empty or not.

Here, his poor virgin Muse
made her start, a street *demoiselle*.
They said: What's she got to sell?

—Nothing.—She stood there, confused,
not hearing the emptiness cry
and watching the wind go by . . .

PARIS

(ii)

Là: vivre à coups de fouet! — passer
En fiacre, en correctionnelle;
Repasser à la ritournelle,
Se dépasser, et trépasser!...

— Non, petit, il faut commencer
Par être grand — simple ficelle —,
Pauvre: remuer l'or à la pelle;
Obscur: un nom à tout casser!...

Le coller chez les mastroquets,
Et l'apprendre à des perroquets
Qui le chantent ou qui le sifflent...

— Musique! — C'est le paradis
Des mahomets et des houris,
Des dieux souteneurs qui se giflent!

PARIS

(ii)

What! pass a lifetime under the knout?
Ride in the 'wagon,' be haled into court,
play that passage yet once more,
surpass yourself, and at last pass out! ...

—No, little guy, you must begin
by being a big shot—a simple trick,—
you're poor: make money, scoop it in;
unknown: then get a big name quick! ...

Placard the bars and public places,
teach it to all the parakeets
that will whistle and sing it to proclaim it ...

—Strike up!—This is the paradise
of houris and followers of Mohammed,
of pimp-gods who slap each other's faces!

PARIS

(v)

C'est la bohême, enfant: renie
Ta lande et ton clocher à jour,
Les mornes de ta colonie
Et les *bamboulas* au tambour.

Chanson usée et bien finie,
Ta jeunesse... Eh, c'est bon un jour!...
Tiens: — c'est toujours neuf — calomnie
Tes pauvres amours... et l'amour.

Evohé! ta coupe est remplie!
Jette le vin, garde la lie...
Comme ça. — Nul n'a vu le tour.

Et qu'un jour le monsieur candide
De toi dise: — Infect! Ah splendide! —
... Ou ne dise rien. — C'est plus court.

PARIS
(v)

This is Bohemia, child: deny
your homeland with its hillocks green,
the heath and the bell-tower pricked with sky,
and *bamboulas* danced to the tambourine.

A song threadbare and out of date,
your youth . . . Ah, that's ephemeral stuff! . . .
But it's always new!—calumniate
your sorry love-affairs . . . and love.

Evoë! your cup is full of wine!
Toss it out, but keep the dregs—be quick,
like that!—Nobody saw the trick.

And sometime may a man of candor
say of you:—Got a dose! That's fine!—
. . . or not say anything.—That's shorter.

PARIS
(vii)

Donc, la *tramontane* est montée;
Tu croiras que c'est arrivé!
Cinq-cent millième Prométhée,
Au roc de carton peint rivé.

Hélas: quel bon oiseau de proie,
Quel vautour, quel *Monsieur Vautour*
Viendra mordre à ton petit foie
Gras, truffé? pour quoi? — Pour le four!...

Four banal!... Adieu la curée! —
Ravalant ta rate rentrée,
Va, comme le pélican blanc,

En écorchant le chant du cygne,
Bec jaune, te percer le flanc...
Devant un pêcheur à la ligne.

PARIS

(vii)

Riding the wind! Hurray! Success!
You'll imagine you're the cock o' the walk!
Five-hundred-thousandth Prometheus,
chained to a painted cardboard rock.

Alas! what bird of prey, what raven,
what vulture, *Monsieur Vautour,* will ever
come to peck at your fat little liver
stuffed with truffles? for what?—For the oven! . . .

The community oven! . . . Good-bye, career!—
Swallowing your stifled spleen,
go, like the white pelican,

croaking your swan-song as you spear,
yellow-beak, your bleeding flank . . .
before some angler on the bank.

PARIS
(viii)

Tu ris. — Bien! — Fais de l'amertume
Prends le pli, Méphisto blagueur,
De l'absinthe! et ta lèvre écume...
Dis que cela vient de ton cœur.

Fais de toi ton œuvre posthume,
Châtre l'amour... l'amour — longueur!
Ton poumon cicatrisé hume
Des miasmes de gloire, ô vainqueur!

Assez, n'est-ce pas? va-t'en!
                     Laisse
Ta bourse — dernière maîtresse —
Ton revolver — dernier ami...

Drôle de pistolet fini!
... Ou reste, et bois ton fond de vie,
Sur une nappe desservie...

PARIS

(viii)

You laugh.—All right!—Make bitter quips,
Mephisto the hoaxer, play your part
with the absinthe! and the froth on your lips . . .
but say it comes straight from your heart.

Prepare your posthumous work in detail,
castrate love . . . love—that bore!
Cicatrized, your lungs inhale
miasmas of glory, O conqueror!

Enough? get out, then! but leave both
the last mistress—that's your purse—
and your revolver—the last friend . . .

odd fish, who has reached an end!
. . . or stay, and drink life's dregs, or worse,
over the cleared-off tablecloth . . .

EPITAPHE

Il se tua d'ardeur, ou mourut de paresse.
S'il vit, c'est par oubli; voici qu'il se laisse:

— Son seul regret fut de n'être pas sa maîtresse. —

Il ne naquit par aucun bout,
Fut toujours poussé vent-debout
Et fut un arlequin-ragoût,
Mélange adultère du tout.

Du *je-ne-sais-quoi,* — mais ne sachant où;
De l'or, — mais avec pas le sou;
Des nerfs, — sans nerf; vigueur sans force;
De l'élan, — avec une entorse;
De l'âme, — et pas de violon;
De l'amour, — mais pire étalon.
— Trop de noms pour avoir un nom. —

Coureur d'idéal, — sans idée;
Rime riche, — et jamais rimée;
Sans avoir été, — revenu;
Se retrouvant partout perdu.

Poète, en dépit de ses vers;
Artiste sans art, — à l'envers;
Philosophe, — à tort à travers.

Un drôle sérieux, — pas drôle.
Acteur, il ne sut pas son rôle;
Peintre: il jouait de la musette;
Et musicien: de la palette.

EPITAPH

He killed himself with zeal, or died of laziness.
It was thoughtless of him to live; he leaves but this:

—His one regret was not to have been his own mistress.—

He was born neither head nor hind first,
by a head-wind was always forced,
and was a save-all ragout,
everything tossed in a stew.

Of *je-ne-sais-quoi,*—but no bent;
gold,—but never a cent;
nerves,—without nerve; slack force;
verve,—with a twisted shin;
soul,—and no violin;
love,—but the worst studhorse.
—Too many names to have one.—

Planless, he chased the sublime;
rime riche,—and never a rhyme;
without having been,—all spent;
he felt lost wherever he went.

Poet, in spite of his verse;
artless artist,—inverse;
philosopher,—random, perverse.

A solemn clown,—not droll.
Actor, did not know his rôle;
painter: he played the musette;
musician: he played the palette.

Une tête! — mais pas de tête;
Trop fou pour savoir être bête;
Prenant pour un trait le mot *très*.
— Ses vers faux furent ses seuls vrais.

Oiseau rare — et de pacotille;
Très mâle... et quelquefois très *fille;*
Capable de tout, — bon à rien;
Gâchant bien le mal, mal le bien.
Prodigue comme était l'enfant
Du Testament, — sans testament.
Brave, et souvent, par peur du plat,
Mettant ses deux pieds dans le plat.

Coloriste enragé, — mais blême;
Incompris... — surtout de lui-même;
Il pleura, chanta juste faux;
— Et fut un défaut sans défauts.

Ne fut *quelqu'un,* ni quelque chose.
Son naturel était la *pose.*
Pas poseur, posant pour *l'unique;*
Trop naïf, étant trop cynique;
Ne croyant à rien, croyant tout.
— Son goût était dans le dégoût.

A head!—but completely vapid;
too mad to know how to be stupid;
for strokes of style, used *very*'s.
—His false were his only true verses.

Pearl of price—cheap paste pearl;
very male . . . and at times very *girl;*
all-capable,—no good at all;
botching good badly, bad well.
Like the Testament's Prodigal Son,—
though testament he had none.
Shunning boldly the commonplace,
often got his foot in his face.

Mad colorist,—but dim;
enigma . . . —above all, to him;
he wept, he sang true-false;
—was a default without defaults.

Being *no one,* nor anything, he
was *pose* essentially.
No poser, he posed as *unique;*
too naïve, being too much the cynic;
believing all, trusting in nothing.
—With gusto he chose the disgusting.

Trop cru, — parce qu'il fut trop cuit,
Ressemblant à rien moins qu'à lui,
Il s'amusa de son ennui,
Jusqu'à s'en réveiller la nuit.
Flâneur au large, — à la dérive,
Epave qui jamais n'arrive...

Trop *Soi* pour se pouvoir souffrir,
L'esprit à sec et la tête ivre,
Fini, mais ne sachant finir,
Il mourut en s'attendant vivre
Et vécut s'attendant mourir.

Ci-gît, —cœur sans cœur, mal planté,
Trop réussi — comme *raté*.

Overcooked, but half-baked, he resembled
nothing less than the self he dissembled.
His ennui amused him all right,
even waking him up at night.
Derelict, drifter,—in short,
a wreck that never makes port . . .

Too much *Himself* to stand it,
dried wits and drunken head,
done, didn't know how to end it,
ready to live, died instead,
and lived prepared to be dead.

Here lies,—heartless heart, a man
too successful—as a *flash in the pan.*

LES AMOURS JAUNES

A L'ETERNEL MADAME

Mannequin idéal, tête-de-turc du leurre,
Eternel Féminin!... repasse tes fichus;
Et viens sur mes genoux, quand je marquerai l'heure,
Me montrer comme on fait chez vous, anges déchus.

Sois pire, et fais pour nous la joie à la malheure,
Piaffe d'un pied léger dans les sentiers ardus,
Damne-toi, pure idole! et ris! et chante! et pleure,
Amante! et meurs d'amour!... à nos moments perdus.

Fille de marbre, en rut! sois folâtre!... et pensive.
Maîtresse, chair de moi! fais-toi vierge et lascive...
Féroce, sainte, et bête, en me cherchant un cœur...

Sois femelle de l'homme, et sers de Muse, ô femme,
Quand le poète brame en *Ame,* en *Lame,* en *Flamme!*
Puis — quand il ronflera — viens baiser ton Vainqueur!

TO THE ETERNAL FEMININE

Figmental mannequin, Turk's-head for the trap,
Eternal Feminine! . . . smooth out your fichus;
and when I say it's time, come to my lap,
show me, *chez* fallen angels, what they do.

Be worse than they, make us joy that goes awry;
with nimble feet prance up the arduous climb,
damn yourself, pure idol! laugh! sing! cry!
belov'd! and die for love . . . in our spare time.

Marble girl! in rut! act crazy! . . . have sport! . . .
be pensive, mistress, my flesh! be virgin and whore . . .
savage, holy, and stupid, to find me a heart . . .

Be female to the male, his Muse, and when
the poet bells: *Ame! Lame! Flamme!* ah, then—
when he snores—come kiss your Conqueror!

FEMININ SINGULIER

Eternel Féminin de l'éternel Jocrisse!
Fais-nous sauter, pantins: nous payons les décors!
Nous éclairons la rampe... Et toi, dans la coulisse,
Tu peux faire au pompier le pur don de ton corps.

Fais claquer sur nos dos le fouet de ton caprice,
Couronne tes genoux!... et nos têtes dix-cors;
Ris! montre tes dents!... mais... nous avons la police,
Et quelque chose en nous d'eunuque et de recors.

... Ah, tu ne comprends pas?... — Moi non plus — Fais la belle,
Tourne: nous sommes soûls! Et plats. Fais la cruelle!
Cravache ton pacha, ton humble serviteur!...

Après, sache tomber! — mais tomber avec grâce —
Sur notre sable fin ne laisse pas de trace!...
— C'est le métier de femme et de gladiateur. —

FEMININE SINGULAR

Eternal Feminine to the eternal Noddy!
make us jacks jump: we pay for everything!
it's we that turn up the lights . . . while you, in the wing,
can make the fireman an outright gift of your body.

Crack on our backs the whip of your caprice,
crown your knees . . . and our heads like a stag of ten;
grin! show your teeth! . . . but . . . we've got the police,
and in us something of eunuch and bailiff's man.

. . . So you don't get it? . . . —Nor I—But give us a whirl,
put on an act: we're plastered, so you can be
cruel and beat your pasha, your servant, me! . . .

Afterward, know how to fall!—but fall with grace—
on the sand of our arena leave no trace! . . .
—That's the business of both gladiator and girl.—

49

BONNE FORTUNE ET FORTUNE

Odor della feminita.

Moi, je fais mon trottoir, quand la nature est belle,
Pour la passante qui, d'un petit air vainqueur,
Voudra bien crocheter, du bout de son ombrelle,
Un clin de ma prunelle ou la peau de mon cœur...

Et je me crois content — pas trop! — mais il faut vivre:
Pour promener un peu sa faim, le gueux s'enivre...

Un beau jour — quel métier! — je faisais, comme ça,
Ma croisière. — Métier!... — Enfin, Elle passa.
— Elle qui? — La Passante! Elle, avec son ombrelle!
Vrai valet de bourreau, je la frôlai... — mais Elle

Me regarda tout bas, souriant en dessous,
Et... me tendit sa main, et...
                                    m'a donné deux sous.
                                    (Rue des Martyrs.)

GOOD FORTUNE AND FORTUNE

Odor della feminita.

I go streetwalking when the weather's fair,
hunting that girl with the slightly triumphant air
who'd like to flick a wink from my eyeball,
or the skin from my heart, with the tip of her parasol . . .

And I think I'm content—not too much!—But one must try:
to cheat his hunger a little, the begger gets high . . .

One fine day—what a life!—I made, as you see,
my little cruise.—What a business! . . . —And then, She passed.
—What She?—That Stroller, with her parasol, at last!
Hangman's helper, I nudged her a bit . . . but She,

from lowered lids, and smiling, slightly amused,
eyed me . . . put out her hand, and . . .

gave me two sous.

(Rue des Martyrs.)

A UNE CAMARADE

Que me veux-tu donc, femme trois fois fille?...
Moi que te croyais un si bon enfant!
— De l'amour?... — Allons: cherche, apporte, pille!
M'aimer aussi, toi!... moi qui t'aimais tant!

Oh! je t'aimais comme... un lézard qui pèle
Aime le rayon qui cuit son sommeil...
L'Amour entre nous vient battre de l'aile:
— Eh! qu'il s'ôte de devant mon soleil!

Mon amour, à moi, n'aime pas qu'on l'aime;
Mendiant, il a peur d'être écouté...
C'est un lazzarone enfin, un bohème,
Déjeunant de jeûne et de liberté.

— Curiosité, bibelot, bricolle?...
C'est possible: il est rare — et c'est son bien. —
Mais un bibelot cassé se recolle;
Et lui, décollé, ne vaudra plus rien!...

Va, n'enfonçons pas la porte entr'ouverte
Sur un paradis déjà trop rendu!
Et gardons à la pomme, jadis verte,
Sa peau, sous son fard de fruit défendu.

Que nous sommes-nous donc fait l'un à l'autre?...
— Rien... — Peut-être alors que c'est pour cela;
Quel a commencé? — Pas moi, bon apôtre!
Après, quel dira: c'est donc tout — voilà!

TO A COMRADE

What do you want of me, woman three times whore? . . .
me who thought you so nice a girl to know!
—Love? . . . —Come on: try, pillage, and explore!
You love me too! . . . me, who loved you so!

Oh, I loved you as . . . a lizard, when it sheds,
loves the rays of light that cook its sleep . . .
Love comes between us, beating wings that keep
the sunlight from me with his hovering shade!

My stubborn heart wants none to love him; beggar,
he fears that someone may overhear him, see . . .
he's only a bum, really, a lazy cadger
who breakfasts on fasting and on liberty.

—Curiosity, bibelot, artifact? . . .
Maybe: he's rare—and that is all he's got.—
But a trinket can be glued up if it cracks;
once he's unglued, he's just a worthless pot! . . .

But let's not force the partly opened door
into a paradise already worn out!
Let's guard this apple's skin, so green before,
shining with the lure of forbidden fruit.

What have we done to each other? . . . —Nothing . . . —Well,
maybe that's the reason we're like this;
who began it?—Not me, sophist! Who can tell
afterwards? Anyhow, that's how it is!

53

— Tous les deux, sans doute... — Et toi, sois bien sûre
Que c'est encor moi le plus attrapé:
Car si, par erreur, ou par aventure,
Tu ne me trompais... je serais trompé!

Appelons cela: *l'amitié calmée;*
Puisque l'amour veut mettre son holà.
N'y croyons pas trop, chère mal-aimée...
— C'est toujours trop vrai, ces mensonges-là! —

Nous pourrons, au moins, ne pas nous maudire,
Si ça t'est égal — le quart d'heure après.
Si nous en mourons — ce sera de rire...
Moi qui l'aimais tant ton rire si frais!

—Both of us, no doubt . . . —You can be sure
that I am still the one who is more misled;
for if, by some mistake or chance, my dear,
you shouldn't deceive me . . . I would still be had!

Let's call it off, then, and just be *good friends,*
since love now wants to make his last halloo.
My misloved darling, don't believe love ends
so easily . . . —These lies are always true!—

We oughtn't curse each other, anyway—
don't you agree?—a quarter-hour after.
If we die of it, the laugh's on us, I'd say . . .
I who have loved so much your fresh young laughter!

UN JEUNE QUI S'EN VA

Morire.

Oh le printemps! — je voudrais paître!...
C'est drôle, est-ce pas: les mourants
Font toujours ouvrir leur fenêtre,
Jaloux de leur part de printemps!

Oh le printemps! Je veux écrire!
Donne-moi mon bout de crayon
— Mon bout de crayon, c'est ma lyre —
Et — là — je me sens un rayon.

Vite!... j'ai vu, dans mon délire,
Venir me manger dans la main
La Gloire qui voulait mè lire!
— La Gloire n'attend pas demain. —

Sur ton bras, soutiens ton poète,
Toi, sa Muse, quand il chantait,
Son Sourire quand il mourait,
Et sa Fête... quand c'était fête.

Sultane, apporte un peu ma pipe
Turque, incrustée en faux saphir,
Celle qui *va bien à mon type*...
Et ris! — C'est fini de mourir;

Et viens sur mon lit de malade;
Empêche la mort d'y toucher,
D'emporter cet enfant maussade
Qui ne veut pas s'aller coucher.

56

A YOUNG MAN GOING

Morire.

Oh, the spring!—I want to graze . . .
Now isn't this a droll thing,
that the dying must have their windows
open to share the spring!

Oh, the spring! I want to write!
—My pencil, that's my lyre—
Give me my stub of a pencil—
there—I feel inspired.

Quick! . . . I've seen in my frenzy
Glory coming to eat
from my hand, she wanted to read me!
—And Glory does not wait.—

Support on your arm your poet,
You, always his Inspiration,
his Smile when he was dying,
his Fête . . . when there was occasion.

Sultana, bring for a moment
my Turkish glass-jeweled pipe,
it perfectly suits my type . . .
and laugh!—Here's an end of dying;

sit by my sickbed; keep
death's fingers off, don't let
them snatch this peevish child
who hates to go to bed.

Ne pleure donc plus, — je suis bête —
Vois: mon drap n'est pas un linceul...
Je chantais cela pour moi seul...
Le vide chante dans ma tête...

Retourne contre la muraille,
— Là — l'esquisse — un portrait de toi.
Malgré lui mon œil soûl travaille
Sur la toile... C'était de moi.

J'entends — bourdon de la fièvre —
Un chant de berceau me monter:
«*J'entends le renard, le lièvre,*
Le lièvre, le loup chanter.»

... Va! nous aurons une chambrette
Bien fraîche, à papier bleu rayé;
Avec un vrai bon lit honnête
A nous, à rideaux... et payé!

Et nous irons dans la prairie
Pêcher à la ligne tous deux,
Ou bien *mourir pour la patrie!*...
— Tu sais, je fais ce que tu veux.

... Et nous aurons des robes neuves,
Nous serons riches à bâiller
Quand j'aurai revu *mes épreuves!*
— Pour vivre, il faut bien travailler...

Don't cry any more,—I'm a fool—
look: it's no shroud, my spread . . .
I was singing this just for myself . . .
the void sings in my head . . .

Turn face to the wall that sketch,
a portrait of you, as you see.
My groggy eyes can't help working
on the canvas . . . done by me.

I hear—the bourdon of fever—
a lullaby that rings:
"I hear the fox, the hare,
the hare, the wolf that sings."

. . . Forget it! We'll have a small attic,
cool, with blue-striped paper;
with a decent bed for two,
with curtains . . . and all paid for!

And we'll go out in the fields,
we two, with a line, to fish,
or even *to die for our country!* . . .
—You know I do what you wish.

And we'll have fine new clothes,
we shall be rich as thieves
when I shall have read *my proofs!*
—A man must work, to live . . .

— Non! mourir...
                La vie était belle
Avec toi, mais rien ne va plus...
A moi le pompon d'immortelle
Des grands poètes que j'ai lus!

A moi, *Myosotis! Feuille morte*
De *Jeune malade à pas lent!*
Souvenir de soi... qu'on emporte
En croyant le laisser — souvent!

— Décès: Rolla: — l'Académie, —
Murger, Baudelaire: — hôpital, —
Lamartine: — en perdant la vie
De sa fille, en strophes pas mal...

Doux bedeau, pleureuse en lévite,
Harmonieux tronc des *moissonnés,*
Inventeur de la *larme écrite,*
Lacrymatoire d'abonnés!...

Moreau — j'oubliais — Hégésippe,
Créateur de l'art-hôpital...
Depuis, j'ai la phtisie en grippe;
Ce n'est plus même original.

— Escousse encor: mort en extase
De lui; mort phtisique d'orgeuil.
— Gilbert: phtisie et paraphrase
Rentrée, en se pleurant *à l'œil.*

—No! to die . . .
                        How fine life was
with you, but those times have sped . . .
mine, the pompon of immortelles
of those great poets I've read.

Mine, *Myosotis! Dead leaf*
of *Jack-with-one-foot-in-the-grave!*
one's souvenir . . . taken along,
which one thought—often!—to leave.

—Dead: Rolla,—the Academy;
Murger, Baudelaire,—the wards;
Lamartine,—of losing his daughter's
life, in strophes of sorts . . .

Mild beadle, gowned weeper, *tuneful*
collection-box for *the mown,*
the *written tear's* inventor,
tear-jar (the subscriber's own).

Moreau—I forgot—Hégésippe,
style-setter for hospital art . . .
since him, I detest consumption;
it's no longer even smart.

—Escousse too: dead of self-praise
and pride, as of T.B.
—Gilbert: of phthisis and ingrown
paraphrase, self-wept (*for free*).

— Un autre incompris: Lacenaire,
Faisant des vers en amateur
Dans le goût anti-poitrinaire,
Avec Sanson pour éditeur.

— Lord Byron, gentleman-vampire,
Hystérique du ténébreux;
Anglais sec, cassé par son rire,
Son noble rire de lépreux.

— Hugo: l'homme apocalyptique,
L'Homme-ceci-tûra-cela,
Meurt, garde national épique!
Il n'en reste qu'un — celui-là! —

Puis... un tas d'amants de la lune,
Guère plus morts qu'ils n'ont vécu,
Et changeant de fosse commune
Sans un discours, sans un écu!

J'en ai lu mourir!... Et ce cygne
Sous le couteau du cuisinier
— Chénier... — Je me sens — mauvais signe!
De la jalousie. — O métier!

Métier! Métier de mourir...
Assez, j'ai fini mon étude.
Métier: se rimer finir!...
C'est une affaire d'habitude.

—One other not understood:
Lacenaire, amateur
in a style non-tubercular,
with Samson for publisher.

—Lord Byron, gentleman-ghoul,
hysteric of the somber;
a Briton, dry and shaken
by his noble, leprous laughter.

—Hugo: apocalypse-man,
the Man of This-will-end-that,
dies, an epic national guard!
There's only one Hugo—he's that!

Then . . . a heap of moon-lovers,
unborn they'd be scarce more dead,
changing one Potter's Field for another
without speeches or cash—not a red!

I've *read* them die! . . . And that swan
under the kitchen knife
—Chénier . . . —I feel, a bad sign,
jealous.—Oh, what a life!

Career! A career of dying . . .
enough, here's my étude.
Career: making rhymes to end with! . . .
it's a matter of habitude.

Mais non la poésie est: vivre,
Paresser encore, et souffrir
Pour toi, maîtresse! et pour mon livre;
Il est là qui dort
                    — Non: mourir!

.   .   .   .

Sentir sur ma lèvre appauvrie
Ton dernier baiser se gercer,
La mort dans tes bras me bercer...
Me déshabiller de la vie!...

                              (Charenton. — Avril.)

But poetry doesn't mean: live,
still idly, suffer as I
for you, mistress! and my book
that's asleep there
               —No, it means: die!

. . . .

It's to feel on my famished lips
your last, chapped kiss, the throes
of death in your cradling arms . . .
to strip off life's old clothes! . . .
                       (Charenton.—April.)

LE POETE CONTUMACE

Sur la côte d'ARMOR. — Un ancien vieux couvent,
Les vents se croyaient là dans un moulin-à-vent,
   Et les ânes de la contrée,
Au lierre râpé venaient râper leurs dents
Contre un mur si troué que, pour entrer dedans,
   On n'aurait pu trouver l'entrée.

— Seul — mais toujours debout avec un rare aplomb,
Crénelé comme la mâchoire d'une vieille,
Son toit à coup de poing sur le coin de l'oreille,
Aux corneilles bayant, se tenait le donjon.

Fier toujours d'avoir eu, dans le temps, sa légende...
Ce n'était plus qu'un nid à gens de contrebande,
Vagabonds de nuit, amoureux buissonniers,
Chiens errants, vieux rats, fraudeurs et douaniers.

— Aujourd'hui l'hôte était, de la borgne tourelle,
Un Poète sauvage, avec un plomb dans l'aile;
Et tombé là parmi les antiques hiboux
Qui l'estimaient d'en haut. — Il respectait leurs trous, —
Lui, seul hibou payant, comme son *bail* le porte:
Pour vingt-cinq écus l'an, dont: remettre une porte. —

Pour les gens du pays, il ne les voyait pas:
Seulement, en passant, eux regardaient d'en bas,
   Se montrant du nez sa fenêtre;
Le curé se doutait que c'était un lépreux;
Et le maire disait: — Moi, qu'est-ce que j'y peux,
   C'est plutôt un Anglais... un *Etre.*

66

THE CONTUMACIOUS POET

On ARMORICA's seacoast.—An ancient former convent;
the winds, which thought it a windmill, came and went,
      and the donkeys of the country
wore down their teeth on the worn-out ivy stalks
on a wall so full of holes that one could walk
      right in without hunting the entry.

Alone—but upright with aplomb most rare,
its crenellations like an old woman's jaws,
gaping wide at the moon, the tower rose,
its roof by blows of a fist knocked over one ear.

Of having its old-time legend always proud . . .
it was nothing now but a nest for the contraband-crowd,
nocturnal vagabonds, the loving snugglers
in bushes, stray dogs, old rats, revenuers, and smugglers.

—Today this one-eyed tower had as its guest
an unsociable Poet, his wings weighed down with lead;
among the elderly owls he'd tumbled there,
and they sized him up from above.—He respected their nests,—
he, the one paying owl, as his *lease* read:
For twenty-five écus a year: and replace the door.—

He never saw the neighbor-folk, although
when they went past they'd stare up from below,
      at his window pointing their nose;
the priest surmised that he was a leper, no doubt;
and the mayor said:—Me! what can I do about
      the *creature?* . . . English, I suppose.

Les femmes avaient su — sans doute par les buses —
Qu'il *vivait en concubinage avec des Muses!*...
Un hérétique enfin... Quelque *Parisien*
De Paris, ou d'ailleurs? — Hélas! on n'en sait rien. —
Il était invisible; et, comme *ses Donzelles*
Ne s'affichaient pas trop, on ne parla plus d'elles.

— Lui, c'était simplement un long flâneur, sec, pâle;
Un ermite-amateur, chassé par la rafale...
Il avait trop aimé les beaux pays malsains.
Condamné des huissiers, comme des médecins,
Il avait posé là, soûl et cherchant sa place
Pour mourir seul ou pour vivre par contumace...

   Faisant, d'un à peu près d'artiste,
   Un philosophe d'à peu près,
   Râleur de soleil ou de frais,
   En dehors de l'humaine piste.

Il lui restait encore un hamac, une vielle,
Un barbet qui dormait sous le nom de *Fidèle;*
Non moins fidèle était, triste et doux comme lui,
Un autre compagnon qui s'appelait l'Ennui.

Se mourant en sommeil, il se vivait en rêve,
Son rêve était le flot qui montait sur la grève,
   Le flot qui descendait;
Quelquefois, vaguement, il se prenait attendre...
Attendre quoi... le flot monter — le flot descendre —
   Ou l'Absente... Qui sait?

The women had learned—no doubt from buzzard-news—
that *he lived in concubinage with the Muse!* . . .
Some *Parisian* from Paris . . . in short, an infidel
from somewhere or other?—Alas, no one could tell.—
He was invisible; *his Wenches, they*
didn't publish their presence, there was no more to say.

—He was merely a skinny loafer, dried-up, pale;
an amateur hermit, blown in by the gale . . .
he had loved too well fine lands where fevers brew.
Condemned by bailiffs, and by doctors too,
he'd perched there, fed up, hunting a place to halt
and die alone, or live on by default . . .

       making almost a philosopher
       of an artist only by half,
       a noon-and-evening grumbler
       aside from the human path.

He still had a hammock and a hurdy-gurdy,
a sleepy spaniel—"Faithful" was his name;
and another pal called "Ennui," just as sturdy
in devotion and as melancholy and tame.

Dying in sleep, in dreams he lived the most,
his dream being the tide that climbed the coast,
       the tide that ebbs and flows;
sometimes, vaguely, he would wait . . . what for? . . .
the tide to come in—the tide to ebb from shore—
       or the Absent One . . . who knows?

Le sait-il bien lui-même?... Au vent de sa guérite,
A-t-il donc oublié comme les morts vont vite?
Lui, ce viveur vécu, revenant égaré,
Cherche-t-il son follet, à lui, mal enterré?

— Certe, Elle n'est pas loin, celle après qui tu brames,
O Cerf de Saint-Hubert! Mais ton front est sans flammes.
N'apparais pas, mon vieux, triste et faux déterré...
Fais le mort si tu peux... Car Elle t'a pleuré!

— Est-ce qu'il pouvait, Lui!... n'était-il pas poète...
Immortel comme un autre?... Et dans sa pauvre tête
Déménagée, encore il sentait que les vers
Hexamètres faisaient les cent pas de travers.

— Manque de savoir-vivre extrême — il survivait —
Et — manque de savoir mourir — il écrivait:

«C'est un être passé de cent lunes, ma Chère,
En ton cœur poétique, à l'état légendaire.
Je rime, donc je vis... ne crains pas, c'est *à blanc,*
— Une coquille d'huître en rupture de banc! —
Oui, j'ai beau me palper; c'est moi! Dernière faute —
En route pour les cieux — car ma niche est si haute! —
Je me suis demandé, prêt à prendre l'essor:
Tête ou pile... — Et voilà — je me demande encor... »

Does even he know? . . . Has he forgotten the hurried
flight of the dead on the wind by his sentry-post?
This worn-out playboy, this bewildered ghost,
is he seeking his goblin mate, himself badly buried?

—Sure, She's not far off, she for whom you bellow,
O Stag of Saint Hubert! But you've no flames on your head.
Don't pop out, sad and wrongly dug up, old fellow . . .
act like a corpse if you can . . . for She mourned you as dead!

—But how could He do that? . . . poet, wasn't he . . .
immortal like another? . . . and in his poor head,
with nobody home, he still felt, crookedly,
hexameters marching with a sentry's tread.

—Not knowing how to live, he kept on living—
and not knowing how to die, he went on writing:

"Here's a person who, these many moons, is part
of the legend, Dear, in your poetic heart.
I rhyme, therefore I am . . . never fear, it's a *blank*,
—an oystershell that's being raked from its bank!—
Sure, I have pinched myself; still I am I!
Last error—heaven-bound—for my niche is that high!—
I've kept asking myself: Are you ready for the flight?
Heads or tails . . . —And look—I am asking it yet . . .

«C'est à toi que je fis mes adieux à la vie,
A toi qui me pleuras, jusqu'à me faire envie
De rester me pleurer avec toi. Maintenant
C'est joué, je ne suis qu'un gâteux revenant,
En os et... (j'allais dire en chair). — La chose est sûre.
C'est bien moi, je suis là, — mais comme une rature.»

«Nous étions amateurs de curiosité:
Viens voir *le Bibelot*. — Moi j'en suis dégoûté. —
Dans mes dégoûts surtout, j'ai des goûts élégants;
Tu sais: j'avais lâché la Vie avec des gants;
L'*Autre* n'est pas même à prendre avec des pincettes...
Je cherche au mannequin de nouvelles toilettes.»

«Reviens m'aider: Tes yeux dans ces yeux-là! Ta lèvre
Sur cette lèvre!... Et, là, ne sens-tu pas ma fièvre
— Ma *fièvre de Toi*?... — Sous l'orbe est-il passé
L'arc-en-ciel au charbon par nos nuits laissé?
Et cette étoile?... — Oh! va, ne cherche plus l'étoile
Que tu voulais voir à mon front;
Une araignée a fait sa toile,
Au même endroit — dans le plafond.»

«Je suis un étranger. — Cela vaut mieux peut-être...
— Eh bien! non, viens encore un peu me reconnaître;
Comme au bon saint Thomas, je veux te voir la foi,
Je veux te voir toucher la plaie et dire: — Toi! — »

"It was to you that I bade life good-bye,
   to you who wept over me till finally I
   wanted to stay and weep with you. But now I've lost—
   the game's played out—I'm only an idiot ghost
   with bones and . . . (I was going to say 'flesh').—Past doubt,
   it's me, all right, I'm here,—like a thing rubbed out.

"We were fanciers of curiosity:
   come see the *Bibelot*.—That's not for me.—
   Especially in my dislikes my taste's above
   the average; you know: I chucked Life, wearing gloves;
   the *Other* can't even be touched with tongs, God knows . . .
   I'm eyeing tailor's dummies for new clothes.

"Come back and help me: Your eyes in these eyes!
   Your lips on these! . . . Don't you feel my fever rise—
   my *fever for You?* . . . —Has the rainbow taken flight
   down under, left in cinders by our nights?
   And that star? . . . —That star you wanted to see on my brow,
        forget it, seek it not;
        There's a spider's web there now
        on the ceiling—in the same spot.

"I'm a stranger.—Well, maybe that's for the best . . .
   —You mean that? no, come back, sound me out anew;
   like good Saint Thomas, I must see you test
   your faith as you touch the wound and then say:—You!—

«Viens encor me finir — c'est très gai: De ta chambre,
  Tu verras mes moissons — nous sommes en décembre —
  Mes grands bois de sapins, les fleurs d'or des genêts,
  Mes bruyères d'Armor... — en tas sur les chenets.
  Viens te gorger d'air pur. — Ici j'ai de la brise
  Si franche!... que le bout de ma toiture en frise.
  Le soleil est si doux... — qu'il gèle tout le temps.
  Le printemps... — Le printemps, n'est-ce pas tes vingt ans?
  On n'attend plus que toi, vois: déjà l'hirondelle
  Se pose... en fer rouillé, clouée à ma tourelle. —
  Et bientôt nous pourrons cueillir le champignon...
  Dans mon escalier que dore... un lumignon.
  Dans le mur qui verdoie existe une pervenche
  Sèche. — ... Et puis nous irons à l'eau *faire* la planche
  — Planches d'épave au sec — comme moi — sur ces plages.
  La Mer roucoule sa *Berceuse pour naufrages;*
  Barcarolle du soir... pour les canards sauvages.»

«En *Paul et Virginie,* et virginaux — veux-tu —
  Nous nous mettrons au vert du paradis perdu...
  Ou *Robinson avec Vendredi* — c'est facile:
  La pluie a déjà fait, de mon royaume, une île.»

«Si pourtant, près de moi, tu crains la solitude,
  Nous avons des amis, sans fard: un braconnier;
  Sans compter un caban bleu, qui, par habitude,
  Fait toujours les cent pas et contient un douanier...
  Plus de clercs d'huissier! J'ai le clair de la lune,
  Et des amis pierrots amoureux sans fortune.»

"Come, finish me off—it's amusing: from your chamber
you'll see my harvests—it's already December—
the golden broom-flowers, my great forests of fir,
and, piled on the andirons, my Armorican briar . . . —
Come, gorge on pure air.—Here, I have a breeze
so fresh! . . . it frizzles the edges of my eaves!
The sun is so pleasant . . . —that it's freezing here.
The spring . . . —the spring, isn't that your twenty years?
You're all that's lacking: see that swallow where it
perches . . . in rusty iron, nailed to the turret.—
And soon we can go to my stairs and pick mushrooms . . .
where a candle-end turns all to a golden gloom.
A dry periwinkle on the moss-green flank
of the wall merely exists.— . . . Then we'll *float* like planks
—ship-planks all dried out—same as me—on these rocks.
The Sea croons her *Lullaby for Shipwrecked Folk;*
an evening barcarolle . . . for the wild ducks.

"Like *Paul and Virginia,* and virginal—it would be nice—
we'll live in the green of the lost paradise . . .
or—it's easy—in *Crusoe and Man Friday* style:
rain has already turned my realm to an isle.

"If you're frightened of solitude, here with just me,
we've friends without veneer—one's a poacher, it's true;
without counting a blue coat which, habitually,
makes its rounds and contains a collector of revenue . . .
no more sheriff's clerks! I have moonlight galore,
and some friendly amorous sparrows, very poor.

— «Et nos nuits!... *Belles nuits pour l'orgie à la tour!*...
Nuits à la Roméo! — Jamais il ne fait jour. —
La Nature au réveil — réveil de déchaînée —
Secouant son drap blanc... éteint ma cheminée.
Voici mes rossignols... rossignols d'ouragans —
Gais comme des pinsons — sanglots de chats-huants!
Ma girouette dérouille en haut sa tyrolienne
Et l'on entend gémir ma porte éolienne,
Comme chez saint Antoine en sa tentation...
Oh viens! joli Suppôt de la séduction!»

— «Hop! les rats du grenier dansent des farandoles!
Les ardoises de toit roulent en castagnoles!
Les Folles du logis...

            Non, je n'ai plus de Folles!»

... «Comme je revendrais ma dépouille à Satan
S'il me tentait avec un petit Revenant...
— Toi — je te vois partout, mais comme un voyant blême,
Je t'adore... Et c'est pauvre: adorer ce qu'on aime!
Apparais, un poignard dans le cœur! — Ce sera,
Tu sais bien, comme dans *Inès de la Sierra*...
— On frappe... oh! c'est quelqu'un...

            Hélas! oui, c'est un rat.»

—"And our nights! . . . *Belles nuits pour l'orgie à la tour!* . . .
Nights *à la* Romeo!—Never the sunrise hour.—
Nature at waking—a waking that bursts forth—
throwing aside its white sheet . . . puts out my hearth.
Hear my nightingales . . . hurricane-nightingales—
gay as finches—the brown owl's sobbing wails!
My weathercock rubs the rust from his Tyrolean
yodels, you hear the groans of my Aeolian
hinges, like St. Anthony's at his temptation . . .
Oh, come, my lovely Votaress of seduction!

—"Hup! the attic rats dance farandoles!
The roof tiles roll around like castagnoles!
My Crotchets . . .
                    No, I've no more Folderols!

. . . "How I'd sell Satan back my skin at cost
if he should tempt me with one little Ghost . . .
—You—I see you everywhere, pale seer,
whom I adore . . . and it's flat: to adore what's dear!
Come forth, with a poniard in your heart!—now, that
would be like *Inès de la Sierra,* pat . . .
—A knock . . . someone, no doubt . . .
                                        Alas, yes, a rat.

—«Je rêvasse... et toujours c'est *Toi*. Sur toute chose,
Comme un esprit follet, ton souvenir se pose;
Ma solitude — *Toi!* — Mes hiboux à l'œil d'or:
—*Toi!* Ma girouette folle: oh *Toi!*... — Que sais-je encor...
—*Toi!* mes volets ouvrant les bras dans la tempête...
Une lointaine voix: c'est Ta chanson! — c'est fête!...
Les rafales fouaillant Ton nom perdu — c'est bête —
C'est bête, mais c'est *Toi!* Mon cœur au grand ouvert
   Comme mes volets en pantenne,
   Bat, tout affolé sous l'haleine
   Des plus bizarres courants d'air.»

«Tiens... une ombre portée, un instant, est venue
Dessiner ton profil sur la muraille nue,
Et j'ai tourné la tête... — Espoir ou souvenir —
Ma Sœur Anne, à ta tour, voyez-vous pas venir?...
— Rien! — je vois... je vois, dans la froide chambrette,
Mon lit capitonné de *satin de brouette;*
Et mon chien qui dort dessus — pauvre animal —
... Et je ris... parce que ça me fait un peu mal.»

«J'ai pris, pour t'appeler, ma vielle et ma lyre,
Mon cœur fait de l'esprit — le sot — pour se leurrer...
Viens pleurer, si mes vers ont pu te faire rire;
   Viens rire, s'ils t'ont fait pleurer... »

—"I daydream . . . always it's *You*. Over everything,
your memory hovers on an elfin wing;
my solitude—*You!*—my gold-eyed owls—*You*'re that—
my mad windvane: ah, *You!* . . . —what more do I know?
—*You:* my shutters opening their arms to the blast . . .
a far-off voice: it's Your song!—it's a feast! . . .
the squalls are lashing Your lost name—it's utter
nonsense, but it's *You!* My heart, spread far
      open as my blown shutters,
      beats crazily, under the bizarre
      gusts of the breathing air.

"Look . . . a shadow for an instant falls,
drawing your profile on the naked wall,
and I turn my head . . . —Is it hope, or do I hear—
Ma Sœur Anne, à ta tour, voyez-vous pas venir? . . .
—Nothing!—I see . . . I see, in my cold attic
my bed with its quilting of *best barnyard satin;*
and my dog asleep on it—poor animal—
. . . and I laugh . . . because it makes me a little ill.

"I have taken my hurdy-gurdy and my lyre, to try
to call you back. My heart—that dumb moon-calf—
deludes himself . . . Come weep, if my verse makes you laugh;
      come laugh, if it makes you cry . . .

«Ce sera drôle... Viens jouer à la misère.
D'après nature: — *Un cœur avec une chaumière.* —
... Il pleut dans mon foyer, il pleut dans mon cœur feu.
Viens! Ma chandelle est morte et je n'ai plus de feu.»

◇   ◇   ◇

Sa lampe se mourait. Il ouvrit la fenêtre.
Le soleil se levait. Il regarda sa lettre,
Rit et la déchira... Les petits morceaux blancs,
Dans la brume, semblaient un vol de goélands.

(Penmarc'h — jour de Noël.)

"Come, let's play Poor Man . . . it's a humorous part.
Back to Nature:—*Love in a straw-thatched hut.*—
. . . It rains on my hearth, it rains on my dead heart.
Come! My candle's dead and my fire is out."

✧　✧　✧

His lamp was dying. He opened the window-shutter.
The sun was rising. He looked at his letter,
laughed, and tore it up . . . the little white
pieces in the fog seemed gulls in flight.

(Penmarc'h—Christmas.)

SERENADE DES SERENADES

GUITARE

Je sais rouler une amourette
    En cigarette,
Je sais rouler l'or et les plats!
Et les filles dans de beaux draps!

Ne crains pas de longueurs fidèles:
Pour mules mes pieds ont des ailes;
Voleur de nuit, hibou d'amour,
    M'envole au jour.

Connais-tu Psyché? — Non? — Mercure?...
Cendrillon et son aventure?
— Non? — Eh bien! tout cela, c'est moi:
    Nul ne me voit.

Et je te laisserais bien fraîche
Comme un petit Jésus en crèche,
Avant le rayon indiscret...
    — Je suis si laid! —

Je sais flamber en cigarette
    Une amourette,
Chiffonner et flamber les draps,
Mettre les filles dans les plats!

GUITAR

I know how to roll an amourette
      like a cigarette,
I know how to roll the dupes for their money!
And in fine sheets how to tumble a honey!

Fear no long faithful lingerings:
instead of slippers my feet wear wings;
night-thief, owl of love, at dawn
      I'm gone.

You know Psyche?—No?—Mercury? . . .
Cinderella and her story?
—No?—I'm all of them, that's me:
      whom none can see.

And I'd leave you cool and fresh—no fib—
like a little Jesus in his crib,
before the indiscreet daylight . . .
      —I'm an ugly sight!—

I know how to puff an amourette
      like a cigarette,
how to tear and burn the sheets—ah, yes—
and how to get the girls in a mess!

CHANSON EN *SI*

Si j'étais noble Faucon,
Tournoîrais sur ton balcon...
— Taureau: foncerais ta porte...
— Vampire: te boirais morte...
　　Te boirais!

— Geôlier: lèverais l'écrou...
— Rat: ferais un petit trou...
Si j'étais brise alizée,
Te mouillerais de rosée...
　　Roserais!

Si j'étais gros Confesseur,
Te fouaillerais, ô ma Sœur!
Pour seconde pénitence,
Te dirais ce que je pense...
　　Te dirais...

Si j'étais un maigre Apôtre,
Dirais: «Donnez-vous l'un l'autre,
Pour votre faim apaiser,
Le pain-d'amour: Un baiser.»
　　Si j'étais!...

Si j'étais Frère-quêteur,
Quêterais ton petit cœur
Pour Dieu le Fils et le Père,
L'Eglise leur Sainte-Mère...
　　Quêterais!

SONG IN *SI*

Could I noble Falcon be,
I'd swoop to your balcony . . .
—bull: I'd crash your gate . . .
—vampire: dead, you'd sate
     me with a drink!

—Jailer: the bolt I'd draw . . .
—rat: a small hole I'd gnaw . . .
a fragrant breeze, with dew
I'd steep and dabble you . . .
     turn you pink!

If I were fat Confessor,
I'd whip you, O my Sister!
As second penance, naught
tell you but what I've thought . . .
     and think . . .

Starveling Apostle, I'd preach:
"Give, each unto each,
kisses: thus be fed
with love's daily bread."
     If I could! . . .

If I were begging Friar,
your little heart I'd require
for God the Son and the Father,
the Church their blessèd Mother . . .
     so I would!

Si j'étais Madone riche,
Jetterais bien, de ma niche,
Un regard, un sou béni,
Pour le cantique fini...
        Jetterais!

Si j'étais un vieux bedeau,
Mettrais un cierge au rideau...
D'un goupillon d'eau bénite
L'éteindrais, la vespre dite,
        L'éteindrais!

Si j'étais roide pendu,
Au ciel serais tout rendu:
Grimperais après ma corde,
Ancre de miséricorde,
        Grimperais!

Si j'étais femme... eh, la Belle,
Tu ferais ma Colombelle...
A la porte les galants
Pourraient se percer les flancs...
        Te ferais...

Enfant, si j'étais la duègne
Rossinante qui te peigne,
Señora, si j'étais Toi...
J'ouvrirais au pauvre Moi,
      — Ouvrirais! —

Were I Madonna rich,
I'd send you, from my niche,
a glance, a blessèd sou,
for the canticle sung through,
      the prayer said.

An old beadle, I'd kindle
by the altar-curtain a candle . . .
vespers done, with devout
sprinkler put it out,
      douse it dead!

Stiff hanged man, who's given
everything to heaven,
I'd climb up the rope—
my stay of mercy and hope—
      overhead!

If I were woman . . . You'd be
lovely Colombelle to me . . .
gallants on my stair,
Beauty, in despair
      might stab their sides . . .

Were I the duenna, Girl,
Rosinante combing your curls,
Señora, could I be
You, unto poor Me
      I'd open wide!

RACCROCS

A MA JUMENT SOURIS

Pas d'éperon ni de cravache,
N'est-ce pas, Maîtresse à poil gris...
C'est bon à pousser une vache,
Pas une petite souris.

Pas de mors à ta pauvre bouche:
Je t'aime, et ma cuisse te touche.
Pas de selle, pas d'étrier:
J'agace, du bout de ma botte,
Ta patte d'acier fin qui trotte.
Va: je ne suis pas cavalier...

— Hurrah! c'est à nous la poussière!
J'ai la tête dans ta crinière,
Mes deux bras te font un collier.
— Hurrah! c'est à nous le hallier!

— Hurrah! c'est à nous la barrière!
Je suis emballé: tu me tiens —
Hurrah!... et le fossé derrière...
Et la culbute!... — Femme, tiens!!

TO MY MOUSE-COLORED MARE

No quirt—right?—nor spur,
Mistress with dusky hide . . .
They're for driving a cow, not her,
the little mouse-gray I ride.

In your poor mouth no bit; without bridle,
and neither stirrup nor saddle,
I love you and touch you, dear,
with my thighs. I prod with my boot,
how your delicate steel paws trot!
Giddap! I'm no cavalier . . .

—Now we eat dust! Hurray!
I bury my head in your mane,
my arms are your collar—hurray!
we're for that hedge again!

—Now over the hurdle—blind!
You're running away! Take it slow!
Hurrah! . . . the last ditch behind . . .
we're down! . . . —Woman, whoa!

FRERE ET SŒUR JUMEAUX

Ils étaient tous deux seuls, oubliés là par l'âge...
Ils promenaient toujours tous les deux, à longs pas,
Obliquant de travers, l'air piteux et sauvage...
Et deux pauvres regards qui ne regardaient pas.

Ils allaient devant eux essuyant les risées,
— Leur parapluie aussi, vert, avec un grand bec —
Serrés l'un contre l'autre et roides, sans pensées...
Eh bien, je les aimais — leur parapluie avec! —

Ils avaient tous les deux servi dans les gendarmes:
La Sœur à la *popotte,* et l'Autre sous les armes;
Ils gardaient l'uniforme encor — veuf de galon;
Elle avait la barbiche, et lui le pantalon.

Un dimanche de mai que tout avait une âme,
Depuis le champignon jusqu'au paradis bleu,
Je flânais aux bois seul, — à deux aussi: la femme
Que j'aimais comme l'air... m'en doutant assez peu.

— Soudain, au coin d'un champ, sous l'ombre verdoyante
Du parapluie éclos, nichés dans un fossé,
Mes Vieux Jumeaux, tous deux, à l'aube souriante,
Souriaient rayonnants... quand nous avons passé.

Contre un arbre, le vieux jouait de la musette,
Comme un sourd aveugle, et sa sœur dans un sillon,
Grelottant au soleil, écoutait un grillon
Et remerciait Dieu de son beau jour de fête.

TWIN BROTHER AND SISTER

They two were alone, forgotten by the years . . .
they always walked together, with long steps,
on the bias, with a pitiful shy air . . .
and their poor eyes gazing at nothing at all, perhaps.

They'd go past people, oblivious to their laughter,
— with their big-beaked green umbrella, whatever the weather—
stiffly, not thinking, leaning close . . . and after
that, well, I loved them and their umbrella together!—

In the Gendarmerie they'd both done several stretches:
the Sister as *barracks cook,* and He on the force;
they still had their uniforms—unstriped, of course;
she had the little beard, and he had the breeches.

One Sunday in May when everything had a soul,
from the mushrooms to the paradisal blue,
by myself—with a girl along—I was taking a stroll;
and I loved her like the air . . . my doubts were few.

—Suddenly, in a field's corner, in the green
umbrella's shadow, with a ditch for nest,
my Ancient Twins, as morning smiled on the scene,
together were beaming on us . . . as we passed.

Against a tree, like a blind mute, the old man wheezed
in his bagpipe; in a furrow, shivering away
in sunlight, his sister heard a cricket and praised
the Lord for such a lovely holiday.

— Avez-vous remarqué l'humaine créature
Qui végète loin du vulgaire intelligent,
Et dont l'âme d'instinct, au trait de la figure,
Se lit... — N'avez-vous pas aimé de chien couchant?...

Ils avaient de cela. — De retour dans l'enfance,
Tenant chaud l'un à l'autre, ils attendaient le jour
Ensemble pour la mort comme pour la naissance...
— Et je les regardais en pensant à l'amour...

Mais l'amour que j'avais près de moi voulut rire;
Et moi, pauvre honteux de mon émotion,
J'eus le cœur de crier au vieux duo: Tityre! —

. . . .

Et j'ai fait ces vieux vers en expiation.

—Haven't you noticed how a human creature
that lives far from the clever herd will keep
his soul, by instinct, candid as his features . . .
Haven't you ever loved a dog asleep? . . .

They were like that.—Returning to infancy,
clinging warmly, they waited the going forth
together, just as for the day of their birth . . .
—and I watched them in a tender reverie . . .

but the girl beside me thought them ridiculous;
and I, weak fool ashamed of my emotion,
I had the brass to shout at the old pair: Tityrus!—

.   .   .   .

And I've made these old verses in expiation.

LE CONVOI DU PAUVRE

(Paris, le 30 avril 1873,
Rue Notre-Dame-de-Lorette.)

Ça monte et c'est lourd — Allons, Hue!
— Frères de renfort, votre main?...
C'est trop!... et je fais le gamin;
C'est mon Calvaire cette rue!

Depuis Notre-Dame-Lorette...
— Allons! *la Cayenne* est au bout,
Frère! du cœur! encore un coup!...
— Mais mon âme est dans la charrette:

Corbillard dur à fendre l'âme,
Vers en bas l'attire un aimant;
Et du piteux enterrement
Rit la Lorette notre dame...

C'est bien ça — splendeur et misère! —
Sous le voile en trous a brillé
Un bout du tréteau funéraire:
Cadre d'or riche... et pas payé.

La pente est âpre, tout de même,
Et les stations sont des *fours,*
Au tableau remontant le cours
De l'Elysée à la Bohême...

— Oui, camarade, il faut qu'on sue
Après son harnais et son art!...
Après les ailes: le brancard!
Vivre notre métier — ça tue...

A POOR MAN'S FUNERAL PROCESSION

(Paris, April 30, 1873.
Rue Notre-Dame-de-Lorette.)

It's a hill and this is heavy—Gee up!
—Lend a hand, you standers-by? . . .
It's too much! . . . I'll play the gutter-pup:
For me this street's a Calvary!

From Notre-Dame-Lorette . . . Let's start!
La Cayenne is at the end,
courage! another heave, my friend! . . .
—but my soul is in the little cart:

hearse to break one's spirit, so weighty,
from below, a magnet pulls;
and this pathetic burial
sets laughing la Lorette our lady . . .

That's fine!—misery and splendor!—
through the holes in the pall there sparkles
the end of an undertaker's trestle:
a gilded picture-frame . . . not paid for.

The slope is steep here, just the same,
and all the stations are *oven-hot,*
for a painting making its way from out
on the Elysée to la Bohême . . .

—Yes, friend, one has to sweat on this hill,
under his harness and for his art! . . .
after the wings, the shafts of a cart!
Our calling is a life that kills! . . .

99

Tués l'idéal et le râble!
Hue!... Et le cœur dans le talon!

. . . .

— Salut au convoi misérable
De peintre écrémé du Salon!

— Parmi les martyrs ça te range;
C'est prononcé comme l'arrêt
De Raphaël, peintre au nom d'ange,
Par le Peintre au nom de... Courbet!

It gets your guts, the ideal's slain!
Gee up! . . . And your heart is in your boots!

.   .   .   .

—Skimmed by the Salon! Salute
this painter's wretched funeral train!

—That ranks you among the martyrs;
a judgment as by Raphael, say,
him with the angel's name, but uttered
by that Painter named . . . Courbet!

DEJEUNER DE SOLEIL

Bois de Boulogne, 1er mai.

Au Bois, les lauriers sont coupés,
Mais le *persil* verdit encore;
Au *Serpolet,* petits coupés
Vertueux vont lever l'Aurore...

L'Aurore brossant sa palette:
Kh'ol, carmin et poudre de riz;
Pour faire dire — la coquette —
Qu'on fait bien les ciels à Paris.

Par ce petit-lever de Mai,
Le Bois se croit à la campagne:
Et, fraîchement trait, le champagne
Semble de la mousse de lait.

Là, j'ai vu les *Chère Madame*
S'encanailler avec le frais...
Malgré tout prendre un vrai bain d'âme!
— Vous vous engommerez après. —

... La voix à la note expansive:
— Vous comprenez; voici mon truc:
Je vends mes Memphis, et j'arrive...
— Cent louis!... — Eh, Eh! Bibi... — Mon duc?...

On presse de petites mains:
— Tiens... assez pur cet attelage. —
Même les cochers, au dressage,
Redeviennent simples humains.

BREAKFAST OF SUNSHINE

Bois de Boulogne, May 1st.

In the Bois, the laurels are cut down,
but the *parsley* still is verdurous;
to the Serpolet go the virtuous
carriages to bring in Dawn . . .

Dawn is brushing on her colors;
her palette: kohl, rice powder, carmine.
Coquette, she'd have us tell each other
Paris skies are utterly charming.

By May's 'at home' the Park is led
to think it's pastoral instead;
freshly milked, the champagne seems
like the bubbly froth of cream.

I've seen the 'My dear Madam' ladies
letting their hair down where the shade is . . .
getting a soul-bath, come what might!
—Later you'll primp up, all right.—

. . . That voice, expansive and alive:
—You understand; this is my trick:
I sell my Memphis bonds, and arrive . . .
—A hundred louis! . . . —Eh, Baby . . . —My duke? . . .

Now one presses the little hands:
—Come on . . . this carriage is nice and clean.—
Even the coachmen understand,
by training, how to be human again.

— Encor toi! vieille *Belle-Impure!*
Toujours, les pieds au plat, tu sors,
Dans ce déjeuner de nature,
Fondre un souper à huit ressorts... —

Voici l'école buissonnière:
Quelques maris jaunes de teint,
Et qui *rentrent dans la carrière*
D'assez bonne heure... le matin.

Le lapin inquiet s'arrête,
Un sergent-de-ville s'assied,
Le sportsman promène sa bête,
Et le rêveur la sienne — à pied. —

Arthur même a presque une tête,
Son faux-col s'ouvre matinal...
Peut-être se sent-il poète,
Tout comme *Byron* — son cheval.

Diane au petit galop de chasse
Fait galoper les papillons
Et caracoler sur sa trace,
Son Tigre et les vieux beaux Lions.

Naseaux fumants, grand œil en flamme,
Crins d'étalon: cheval et femme
Saillent de l'avant!...
                                    — Peu poli.
— Pardon: *maritime*... et joli.

—So it's you, old *Belle-Impure!*
Always getting your paws in the platter,
you come to this little breakfast with Nature
ready to pounce on the food, I'm sure . . . —

Look, the truants all come swarming:
sallow husbands *sneaking back*
dutifully to their proper track
plenty early . . . in the morning.

The timorous rabbit stops in its tracks,
a policeman takes a chair,
the sportsman promenades his hack,
and the dreamer his—as he strolls there.—

Even Arthur almost shows a mind,
his morning collar open, of course . . .
perhaps he's poetically inclined,
just like *Byron*—that's his horse.

Off at a hunting canter, Dian's
making the butterflies dance and sail,
while caracoling along her trail
come her Tiger and the grand old Lions.

Nostrils smoking, eyes flame-bright,
manes like a stallion's: woman and steed
saillent de l'avant! . . .
                            —That's hardly polite.
—Pardon: *a sailor's phrase* . . . pretty indeed.

A L'ETNA

Sicelides Musae, paulo majora canamus.

(Virgile.)

Etna — j'ai monté le Vésuve...
Le Vésuve a beaucoup baissé:
J'étais plus chaud que son effluve,
Plus que sa crête hérissé...

— Toi que l'on compare à la femme...
— Pourquoi? — Pour ton âge? — ? ou ton âme
De caillou cuit?... — Ça fait rêver...
— Et tu t'en fais rire à crever! —

— Tu ris jaune et tousses: sans doute,
Crachant un vieil amour malsain;
La lave coule sous la croûte
De ton vieux cancer au sein.

— Couchons ensemble, Camarade!
Là — mon flanc sur ton flanc malade:
Nous sommes frères, par Vénus,
Volcan!...
        Un peu moins... un peu plus...

                 (Palermo. — Août.)

TO MOUNT ETNA

Sicilian Muses, let us now
sing somewhat more nobly.
(*Vergil.*)

Etna—I've climbed Vesuvius . . .
and Vesuvius was a lot depressed:
I was hotter than its effluvia's
gases, than its bristling crest . . .

—They compare you to a woman . . . why?—
Is it for your age?—or for your baked
and flinty soul? . . . What dreams awake . . .
—and you laugh enough to burst and die!—

—You laugh yellow and cough: no doubt
spitting some old lovesickness out;
the lava flows beneath the crust
of your old cancer of the breast.

—Comrade, let us sleep together!
There—my flank upon your sore
flank: by Venus, we're sister and brother,
volcano! . . .
A bit less . . . a bit more . . .

(Palermo.—August.)

HIDALGO!

Ils sont fiers, ceux-là!... comme poux sur la gale!
C'est à la don-juan qu'ils vous *font* votre malle.
Ils ne sentent pas bon, mais ils fleurent le preux:
Valeureux vauriens, crétins chevalereux!
Prenant sans demander — toujours suant la race, —
Et demandant un sol, — mais toujours pleins de grâce...

Là, j'ai fait le croquis d'un mendiant à cheval:
— Le Cid... un cid par un *été* de carnaval.

— Je cheminais — à pieds — traînant une compagne;
Le soleil craquelait la route en blanc d'Espagne;
Et *le cid* fut sur nous en un temps de galop...
Là, me pressant entre le mur et le garrot:
— Ah! seigneur *Cavalier,* d'honneur! sur ma parole!
Je mendie à genoux: un oignon... une obole!... —
(Et son cheval paissait mon col.) — Pauvre animal,
Il vous aime déjà! Ne prenez pas à mal...
— Au large! — Oh! mais: au moins votre bout de cigare!...
La Vierge vous le rende. — Allons: au large! ou: gare!
(Son pied nu prenait ma poche en étrier.)
— Pitié pour un infirme, ô seigneur cavalier...
— Tiens donc un sou... — Señor, que jamais je n'oublie
Votre Grâce! Pardon, je vous ai retardé...
Señora: Merci, toi! pour être si jolie...
Ma Jolie, et: Merci pour m'avoir regardé!

(Cosas de España.)

108

HIDALGO!

They're proud, these people! . . . proud as lice on pocks!
It's with a Don Juan's manners they *pack* your box.
They don't smell good, but they've a scent of the brave:
each knightly crackpot, and each valorous knave!
They take without asking—forever oozing their race,—
and beg a penny—but always with fabulous grace . . .

See, I've sketched here a beggar, horse and all:
—The Cid . . . a cid for an *all-summer* Carnival.

—Afoot, with my woman in tow, I was plodding on;
the road, like chalk, was crackling under the sun;
and *the cid* was upon us, riding hell-for-leather . . .
squeezed me betwixt the wall and his horse's withers:
—Ah, Sir *Knight,* most truly you honor us!
I beg of you, on my knees: an onion . . . an obolus! . . . —
(Meanwhile his horse was nibbling my neck.)—Poor beast,
he loves you already! Don't, pray, be displeased . . .
—Get away!—At least, the butt of your cigar! . . .
and may the Virgin reward you.—Be off, or beware!
(My pocket was stirrup for his naked toes.)
—Sir Cavalier, take pity on my woes . . .
—Here's a sou, then . . . —Señor, may I never forget
Your Grace! And pardon me, that I have kept
you . . . Señora: my thanks that you should be
so lovely, and: thank you for having looked at me!

(Cosas de España.)

ARMOR

PAYSAGE MAUVAIS

Sables de vieux os — Le flot râle
Des glas: crevant bruit sur bruit...
— Palud pâle, où la lune avale
De gros vers pour passer la nuit.

— Calme de peste, où la fièvre
Cuit... Le follet damné languit.
— Herbe puante où le lièvre
Est un sorcier poltron qui fuit...

— La Lavandière blanche étale
Des trépassés le linge sale,
Au *soleil des loups*... — Les crapauds,

Petits chantres mélancoliques,
Empoisonnent de leurs coliques
Les champignons, leurs escabeaux.

(Marais de Guérande. — Avril.)

EVIL LANDSCAPE

Sands of old bones—The wave gasps
knells: breaking sound on sound . . .
—pale salt-marsh, where the moon downs
fat worms to make the night pass.

—Calm of pestilence, where
fever cooks . . . The curs'd marsh-light
dies.—Stinking grass where the hare
is a scared warlock in flight . . .

—The White Laundress spreads
the dirty clothes of the dead,
to the *sun of the wolves* . . . —The toads,

little precentors of gloom,
poison with their bellies' loads
their round stools, the mushrooms.

(Marais de Guérande.—April.)

NATURE MORTE

Des coucous l'*Angelus* funèbre
A fait sursauter, à ténèbre,
Le coucou, pendule du vieux,

Et le chat-huant, sentinelle,
Dans sa carcasse à la chandelle
Qui flamboie à travers ses yeux.

— Ecoute se taire la chouette...
— Un cri de bois: C'est *la brouette*
De la Mort, le long du chemin...

Et, d'un vol joyeux, la corneille
Fait le tour du toit où l'on veille
Le défunt qui s'en va demain.

(Bretagne. — Avril.)

STILL LIFE

The cuckoos' mournful Angelus
has made the old man's clock, at dusk,
start to cuckoo in surprise,

and the wood-owl, sentinel,
with candle in his carcass-shell,
show fire through his startled eyes.

—Hear the hooting owl forbear
to cry . . . —That creak of wood, somewhere
along the road: it's *Death's hand-barrow* . . .

and, in joyous flight, the crow
circles the roof, where they below
watch the dead who leaves tomorrow.

(Brittany.—April.)

LA RAPSODE FORAINE
ET LE PARDON DE SAINTE-ANNE

La Palud, 27 août, jour du Pardon.

❖

Bénite est l'infertile plage
Où, comme la mer, tout est nud.
Sainte est la chapelle sauvage
De Sainte-Anne-de-la-Palud,

De la Bonne Femme Sainte Anne,
Grand'tante du petit Jésus,
En bois pourri dans sa soutane,
Riche... plus riche que Crésus!

Contre elle la petite Vierge,
Fuseau frêle, attend l'*Angelus;*
Au coin, Joseph, tenant son cierge,
Niche, en saint qu'on ne fête plus...

. . . .

C'est le *Pardon.* — Liesse et mystères —
Déjà l'herbe rase a des poux...
— *Sainte Anne, onguent des belles-mères!*
Consolation des époux!...

Des paroisses environnantes:
De Plougastel et Loc-Tudy,
Ils viennent tous planter leurs tentes,
Trois nuits, trois jours, — jusqu'au lundi.

THE ITINERANT RHAPSODIST
AND THE PARDON OF SAINT ANNE

La Palud, August 27, day of the Pardon.

[i]

Blessèd is the sterile shore
where all is bare as the sea and rude.
Holy is the rugged chapel
of Saint Anne of La Palud,

of that kind old woman, good Saint Anne,
great-aunt of the little Jesus,
of rotted wood beneath her robe,
but rich . . . more rich than Croesus!

The little Virgin facing her,
frail distaff, for the Angelus waits;
in the corner, Joseph, holding his candle,
nestles, a saint nobody fêtes . . .

.   .   .   .

It's the Pardon.—Gaiety, mysteries—
there are lice already in the straw . . .
—*Saint Anne, balm of young wives' mothers!*
consolation of sons-in-law!

From the neighboring parishes,
from Plougastel, the folk come swarming,
from Loc-Tudy, to pitch their tents,
three nights, three days, till Monday morning.

117

Trois jours, trois nuits, la palud grogne,
Selon l'antique rituel,
— Chœur séraphique et chant d'ivrogne —
Le CANTIQUE SPIRITUEL.

◇

Mère taillée à coups de hache,
Tout cœur de chêne dur et bon;
Sous l'or de ta robe se cache
L'âme en pièce d'un franc Breton!

— Vieille verte à face usée
Comme la pierre du torrent,
Par des larmes d'amour creusée,
Séchée avec des pleurs de sang!

— Toi, dont la mamelle tarie
S'est refait, pour avoir porté
La Virginité de Marie,
Une mâle virginité!

— Servante-maîtresse altière,
Très haute devant le Très-Haut,
Au pauvre monde, pas fière,
Dame pleine de comme-il-faut!

— Bâton des aveugles! Béquille
Des vieilles! Bras des nouveau-nés!
Mère de madame ta fille!
Parente des abandonnés!

Three days, three nights, the salt-marsh grunts,
faithful to ancient ritual,
—seraphic choir and songs of the drunks—
the Cantique spirituel.

[ii]

Mother hacked out with blows of the hatchet
from the core of an oak tree, fine and hard,
under the gold of your robe is hidden,
all sound Breton too, your heart!

—Green old woman, with face worn
like a stone in the torrent's flood,
furrowed by the tears of love,
drained from weeping tears of blood!

—You, whose dried, exhausted breasts
were refreshed by pregnancy
with the Virginity of Mary,
a male virginity!

Servant-mistress, proud and stately,
high-placed before the Highest Liege:
not arrogant toward these wretched folk,
lady with noblesse oblige!

—Staff of blindmen! Crutch to prop
old women! Arms for the new swaddling!
Mother of Our Lady your daughter!
Foster-parent of the foundling!

— O Fleur de la pucelle neuve!
Fruit de l'épouse au sein grossi!
Reposoir de la femme veuve...
Et du veuf Dame-de-merci!

— Arche de Joachim! Aïeule!
Médaille de cuivre effacé!
Gui sacré! Trèfle quatre-feuille!
Mont d'Horeb! Souche de Jessé!

— O toi qui recouvrais la cendre,
Qui filais comme on fait chez nous,
Quand le soir venait à descendre,
Tenant l'ENFANT sur tes genoux;

Toi qui fus là, seule, pour faire
Son maillot neuf à Bethléem,
Et là, pour coudre son suaire
Douloureux, à Jérusalem!...

Des croix profondes sont tes rides,
Tes cheveux sont blancs comme fils...
— Préserve des regards arides
Le berceau de nos petits-fils!

Fais venir et conserve en joie
Ceux à naître et ceux qui sont nés.
Et verse, sans que Dieu te voie,
L'eau de tes yeux sur les damnés!

—O Flowering of the young virgin!
Fruit of the wife with the swollen womb!
Haven and altar of the widow . . .
Lady of Grace for the widower's gloom!

—Ark of Joachim! Grandam!
Medallion of copper, worn and dim!
Sacred mistletoe! Four-leaved clover!
Mount of Horeb! Of Jesse's stem!

—O you who covered the embers with ashes,
who, when the shades of night were come,
sat with the CHILD upon your knees
and span, as our women do at home;

you who were there, alone, to weave
his swaddling-band at Bethlehem,
and there, to stitch his winding-sheet
grievously, at Jerusalem! . . .

Your wrinkles are crosses of deep affliction,
your hair is white as linen threads . . .
—Protect from dry, unfeeling eyes
our grandsons in their trundle-beds!

The new-born and the yet unborn
summon, and make glad their years.
Without God's ever seeing you,
sprinkle on the damned your tears!

Reprends dans leur chemise blanche
Les petits qui sont en langueur...
Rappelle à l'éternel Dimanche
Les vieux qui traînent en longueur.

— Dragon-gardien de la Vierge,
Garde la crèche sous ton œil.
Que, près de toi, Joseph-concierge
Garde la propreté du seuil!

Prends pitié de la fille-mère,
Du petit au bord du chemin...
Si quelqu'un leur jette la pierre,
Que la pierre se change en pain!

— Dame bonne en mer et sur terre,
Montre-nous le ciel et le port,
Dans la tempête ou dans la guerre...
O Fanal de la bonne mort!

Humble: à tes pieds n'a point d'étoile,
Humble... et brave pour protéger!
Dans la nue apparaît ton voile,
Pâle auréole du danger.

— Aux perdus dont la vie est grise,
(— Sauf respect — perdus de boisson)
Montre le clocher de l'église
Et le chemin de la maison.

Take back again, in their white shirts,
the little ones who pine away . . .
call back the old folks dragging on
to the eternal Sabbath Day.

—Dragon-guardian of the Virgin,
watch the crib with heedful eyes.
Near you, may Joseph the concierge
keep the threshold clean and nice!

Take pity on the girl with a baby,
by the road, a mother though unwed . . .
if anyone casts a stone at them,
may that stone be turned to bread!

—Lady of help on land and sea,
guide us to heaven and the harbor aright,
in time of tempest or in war . . .
to the good death, O Beacon-light!

Humble, with no stars at your feet,
humble . . . but a gallant protector!
in the sky your veil appears to us,
pale aureole of danger.

—To those lost ones whose lives are fuddled
(—saving your presence—they've got a load
of liquor), show the church's belfry
and set them on the homeward road.

Prête ta douce et chaste flamme
Aux chrétiens qui sont ici...
Ton remède de bonne femme
Pour les bêtes-à-corne aussi!

Montre à nos femmes et servantes
L'ouvrage et la fécondité...
— Le bonjour aux âmes parentes
Qui sont bien dans l'éternité!

Nous mettrons un cordon de cire,
De cire-vierge jaune, autour
De ta chapelle et ferons dire
Ta messe basse au point du jour.

— Préserve notre cheminée
Des sorts et du monde malin...
A Pâques te sera donnée
Une quenouille avec du lin.

Si nos corps sont puants sur terre,
Ta grâce est un bain de santé;
Répands sur nous, au cimetière,
Ta bonne odeur de sainteté.

— A l'an prochain! — Voici ton cierge:
(C'est deux livres qu'il a coûté)
... Respects à Madame la Vierge,
Sans oublier la Trinité.

Lend your chaste and gentle flame
to all Christians here below . . .
and your old-woman's remedies
give to the horned beasts also!

Teach our women and our servants
labor and fecundity . . .
—Say Bon jour to our kith and kin
who are quite snug in eternity!

We'll make a ring of yellow wax,
virgin candle-wax, all the way
around your chapel and have low mass
said in your name at break of day.

—Keep, we pray, our hearthsides safe
from malicious folk and evil charms . . .
and, come Easter, you'll be given
a distaff wound with flaxen yarn.

If our bodies stink on earth,
your grace is a bath of health to bless;
shed on us, in the burial ground,
the fragrance of your holiness.

—Now till next year!—Here's your candle:
(two good francs they got of me)
. . . my respects to Our Lady the Virgin,
not forgetting the Trinity.

... Et les fidèles, en chemise,
— *Sainte Anne, ayez pitié de nous!* —
Font trois fois le tour de l'église
En se traînant sur leurs genoux

Et boivent l'eau miraculeuse
Où les Job teigneux ont lavé
Leur nudité contagieuse...
— *Allez: la Foi vous a sauvé!* —

C'est là que tiennent leurs cénacles
Les pauvres, frères de Jésus.
— Ce n'est pas la cour des miracles,
Les trous sont vrais: *Vide latus!*

Sont-ils pas divins sur leurs claies
Qu'auréole un nimbe vermeil,
Ces propriétaires de plaies,
Rubis vivants sous le soleil!...

En aboyant, un rachitique
Secoue un moignon désossé,
Coudoyant un épileptique
Qui travaille dans un fossé.

. . . And the faithful, in their shirts,
—*Saint Anne, pity our miseries!*
crawl three times around the church,
dragging themselves along on their knees,

and drinking the miraculous water
where these Jobs with scurvy have had a bath,
washing their contagious flesh . . .
—*Go: you have been saved by faith!*—

Here come, to meet their coterie,
all the poor, the brothers of Jesus.
—This is no court of miracles,
these holes are real: *Vide latus!*

Aren't they divine there on the stretchers,
haloed with a nimb of vermilion,
these proprietors of sores,
living rubies under the sun! . . .

Yelping, a rachitic fellow
shakes a boneless stump with which
he's elbowing an epileptic
having a spasm in a ditch.

Là, ce tronc d'homme où croît l'ulcère,
Contre un tronc d'arbre où croît le gui;
Ici, c'est la fille et la mère
Dansant la danse de Saint-Guy.

Cet autre pare le cautère
De son petit enfant malsain:
— L'enfant se doit à son vieux père...
— Et le chancre est un gagne-pain!

Là, c'est l'idiot de naissance,
Un *visité par Gabriel,*
Dans l'extase de l'innocence...
— L'innocent est près du ciel! —

— Tiens, passant, regarde: tout passe...
L'œil de l'idiot est resté.
Car il est en état-de-grâce...
— Et la Grâce est l'Éternité! —

Parmi les autres, après vêpre,
Qui sont d'eau bénite arrosés,
Un cadavre, vivant de lèpre,
Fleurit, — souvenir des croisés...

Puis tous ceux que les Rois de France
Guérissaient d'un toucher de doigts...
— Mais la France n'a plus de rois,
Et leur dieu suspend sa clémence.

There, on a man's trunk an ulcer is growing
by a trunk where mistletoe grows on a tree.
Here, it's a mother and daughter dancing
the twitching dances of *Saint-Guy*.

This other is doing a cautery
on a sore for his little tad:
—that chancre is a sure breadwinner . . .
—and the boy owes it all to his old dad!

There, an idiot from birth,
a boon by the angel Gabriel given,
in a simple-minded ecstasy . . .
—a simpleton is near to Heaven!—

—Look, passer-by: all else may pass,
but the idiot's stare will last, for he
is already in a state of grace . . .
—and Grace, that is Eternity!—

After vespers, among the others—
with holy water they've all been sprayed—
blossoms a leper, a living cadaver,—
a souvenir of the Crusades . . .

Next, all those the Kings of France
used to heal by the touch of a finger . . .
—but their God has suspended his clemency,
and there are no French kings any longer.

— Charité dans leurs écuelles!...
Nos aïeux ensemble ont porté
Ces fleurs de lis en écrouelles
Dont ces *choisis* ont hérité.

Miserere pour les ripailles
Des *Ankokrignets* et *Kakous!*...
Ces moignons-là sont des tenailles,
Ces béquilles donnent des coups.

Risquez-vous donc là, gens ingambes,
Mais gare pour votre toison:
Gare aux doigts crochus! gare aux jambes
En *kyriè-éleison!*

... Et détourne-toi, jeune fille,
Qui viens là voir et prendre l'air...
Peut-être, sous l'autre guenille,
Percerait la guenille en chair...

C'est qu'ils chassent là sur leurs terres!
Leurs peaux sont leurs blasons béants:
— Le droit du seigneur à leurs serres!...
Le droit du seigneur de céans! —

Tas d'*ex-voto* de carne impure,
Charniers d'élus pour les cieux,
Chez le Seigneur ils sont chez eux!
— Ne sont-ils pas sa créature?...

—Alms into these beggars' bowls! . . .
All our ancestors have borne
these fleurs-de-lis of scrofula
with which these *chosen ones* are born.

Have mercy, Lord, upon the revels
of *Ankokrignets* and *Kakous!* . . .
These arm-stumps can clutch like pincers,
these crutches beat you black and blue.

Take a chance, you nimble rascals,
but look out for your woolly locks:
beware of shanks at the *Kyrie eleison!*
beware of fingers that are hooks!

. . . Turn aside, young woman, who
would see the sights and take the air . . .
maybe from under rags and tatters
a rag of flesh may prod through a tear . . .

How they go hunting on their lands!
Their skins are their gaping blazonry:
—the *droit du seigneur* in their claws! . . .
the right of the master's property!—

Charnel-house for Heaven's elect,
vile flesh in heaps for immolation,
they're right at home in the house of the Lord
—for aren't they all his own creation? . . .

Ils grouillent dans le cimetière:
On dirait des morts déroutés
N'ayant tiré de sous la pierre
Que des membres mal reboutés.

— Nous, taisons-nous!... Ils sont sacrés.
C'est la faute d'Adam punie.
Le doigt d'En-haut les a marqués:
— La droite d'En-haut soit bénie!

Du grand troupeau, boucs émissaires
Chargés des forfaits d'ici-bas,
Sur eux Dieu purge ses colères!...
— Le pasteur de Sainte-Anne est gras. —

. . . .

⋄

Mais une note pantelante,
Echo grelottant dans le vent,
Vient battre la rumeur bêlante
De ce purgatoire ambulant.

Une forme humaine qui beugle
Contre le *calvaire* se tient;
C'est comme une moitié d'aveugle:
Elle est borgne, et n'a pas de chien...

They come swarming from the graveyard:
one might say, from beneath the stones
the bewildered dead have dragged up nothing
but a mass of mis-set bones.

—Let us be silent! . . . They are sacred.
Adam's sin paid its penalty.
The finger from On High has marked them:
—blest be the hand of the Most High!

As for the big flock, scapegoats laden
with all the sins we're busy at,
on them the wrath of God is vented! . . .
—The pastor of Saint Anne's, he's fat.—

. . . .

[iv]

But now on the wind a panting sound,
an echo shuddering and eerie,
breaks into the bleating murmur
of this wandering purgatory.

A human figure, bellowing,
stands beside the Calvary;
like the half of a blindman, say:
she has no dog and but one eye . . .

C'est une rapsode foraine
Qui donne aux gens pour un liard
L'*Istoyre de la Magdalayne,*
Du *Juif-Errant* ou d'*Abaylar.*

Elle hâle comme une plainte,
Comme une plainte de la faim,
Et, longue comme un jour sans pain,
Lamentablement, sa complainte...

— Ça chante comme ça respire,
Triste oiseau sans plume et sans nid,
Vaguant où son instinct l'attire:
Autour des Bon Dieu de granit...

Ça peut parler aussi, sans doute.
Ça peut penser comme ça voit:
Toujours devant soi la grand'route...
Et, quand ç'a deux sous... ça les boit.

— Femme: on dirait, hélas — sa nippe
Lui pend, ficelée en jupon;
Sa dent noire serre une pipe
Eteinte... — Oh, la vie a du bon! —

Son nom?... ça se nomme Misère.
Ça s'est trouvé né par hasard.
Ça sera trouvé mort par terre...
La même chose — quelque part.

It is a wandering rhapsodist
who gives the people for a sou
the *Story of the Magdalen,*
of *Abelard,* or the *Wandering Jew.*

She drags out, like a long complaint,
or like a hungry man who wails,
as long as a day without any bread,
lamentably, her mournful tales . . .

—A wretched bird, without nest or feathers,
wandering as her whimsies plan it,
she sings as easily as she breathes,
around these *Bon Dieu*'s made of granite . . .

This thing can also speak, no doubt,
and about the same as she sees, can think;
always before her the endless road . . .
when she gets two sous . . . she buys a drink.

Woman? you ask, alas—her rig
hangs on her, petticoat hoicked by a string;
she clenches her black teeth on a pipe
long gone out . . . —Oh, life's the thing!—

Her name? . . . she's known as Misery.
She was born by accident, she found;
and somewhere, sometime—the same way—
she'll be found dead upon the ground . . .

Si tu la rencontres, Poète,
Avec son vieux sac de soldat:
C'est notre sœur... donne — c'est fête —
Pour sa pipe, un peu de tabac!...

Tu verras dans sa face creuse
Se creuser, comme dans du bois,
Un sourire; et sa main galeuse
Te faire un vrai signe de croix.

If you happen to come across her, Poet,
with her old army haversack, oh,
she's our sister . . . —it's a holy day—
give her a pinch of pipe tobacco! . . .

You'll see then, as if dug in wood,
scooped deeper in her furrowed face,
a smile; and with her mangy hand
she'll make you a true sign of the cross.

CRIS D'AVEUGLE

Sur l'air bas-breton: *Ann hini goz.*

L'œil tué n'est pas mort
Un coin le fend encor
Encloué je suis sans cercueil
On m'a planté le clou dans l'œil
L'œil cloué n'est pas mort
Et le coin entre encor

Deus misericors
Deus misericors
Le marteau bat ma tête en bois
Le marteau qui ferra la croix
Deus misericors
Deus misericors

Les oiseaux croque-morts
Ont donc peur à mon corps
Mon Golgotha n'est pas fini
Lamma lamma sabacthani
Colombes de la Mort
Soiffez après mon corps

Rouge comme un sabord
La plaie est sur le bord
Comme la gencive bavant
D'une vieille qui rit sans dent
La plaie est sur le bord
Rouge comme un sabord

THE BLINDMAN'S PLAINT

To a Low Breton air: "Ann hini goz."

    The slain eye is alive
    there is a wedge that rives
spiked without a coffin I
have got a nail smack in the eye
    the nailed eye is alive
    and the wedge still rives

    Deus misericors
    Deus misericors
the hammer is pounding my head of wood
the hammer that will drive iron in the rood
    Deus misericors
    Deus misericors

    My flesh still keeps scared
    the undertaker-birds
Golgotha still goes on for me
Lama lama sabacthani
    doves of Death be ready
    and thirsty for my body

    Like a ship's gun-port the wound
    is rimmed with red around
like the slavering gums of an old crone's mouth
who laughs and her teeth have fallen out
    rimmed with red around
    like a gun-port is the wound

Je vois des cercles d'or
Le soleil blanc me mord
J'ai deux trous percés par un fer
Rougi dans la forge d'enfer
Je vois un cercle d'or
Le feu d'en haut me mord

Dans la moelle se tord
Une larme qui sort
Je vois dedans le paradis
Miserere De profundis
Dans mon crâne se tord
Du soufre en pleur qui sort

Bienheureux le bon mort
Le mort sauvé qui dort
Heureux les martyrs les élus
Avec la Vierge et son Jésus
O bienheureux le mort
Le mort jugé qui dort

Un Chevalier dehors
Repose sans remords
Dans le cimetière bénit
Dans sa sieste de granit
L'homme en pierre dehors
A deux yeux sans remords

Golden rings I see
the white sun tortures me
I have two holes pierced right well
by an iron rod in the forge of hell
golden rings I see
the sky's fire tortures me

From the marrow twists
a teardrop that bursts
I see therein God's paradise
Miserere De profundis
writhing from my skull
tears of sulphur fall

The good dead man is blest
the saved dead man at rest
happy are the martyrs chosen
to be with Jesus and the Virgin
Oh how he is blest
the judged dead man at rest

A Knight out-of-doors
rests without remorse
in the blessèd cemetery
he takes a nap of statuary
the stone man out-of-doors
has eyes without remorse

Ho je vous sens encor
Landes jaunes d'Armor
Je sens mon rosaire à mes doigts
Et le Christ en os sur le bois
A toi je baye encor
O ciel défunt d'Armor

Pardon de prier fort
Seigneur si c'est le sort
Mes yeux deux bénitiers ardents
Le diable a mis ses doigts dedans
Pardon de crier si fort
Seigneur contre le sort

J'entends le vent du nord
Qui bugle comme un cor
C'est l'hallali des trépassés
J'aboie après mon tour assez
J'entends le vent du nord
J'entends le glas du cor

(Menez-Arroz.)

Ah I feel you still
       dun Breton heath and hill
my fingers feel the rosary
and the Christ in bone upon the tree
       I still hanker for
       you dead sky of Armor

       Pardon my prayer overwrought
       Lord if this be my lot
my eyes two burning holy fonts
where the devil stuck his fingers once
       pardon Lord this great
       outcry against fate

       I hear the wind from the north
       that bugles like a horn
it's the mort for all those past return
I yelp enough now for my turn
       I hear the wind from the north
       I hear the knell of its horn

                              (Menez-Arroz.)

GENS DE MER

LE BOSSU BITOR*

Un pauvre petit diable aussi vaillant qu'un autre,
Quatrième et dernier à bord d'un petit *cotre*...
Fier d'être matelot et de manger pour rien,
Il remplaçait le *coq,* le mousse et le chien;
Et comptait, comme ça, quarante ans de service,
Sur le *rôle* toujours inscrit comme *novice!* —

... Un vrai bossu: cou tors et retors, très madré,
Dans sa coque il gardait sa petite influence;
Car chacun sait qu'en mer un bossu porte chance...
— Rien ne f...iche malheur comme femme ou curé!

Son nom: c'était Bitor—nom de mer et de guerre —
Il disait que c'était un tremblement de terre
Qui, jeune et fait au tour, l'avait tout démoli:
Lui, son navire et des cocotiers... au Chili.

. . . .

Le soleil est noyé. — C'est le soir. — Dans le port
Le navire bercé sur ses câbles, s'endort
Seul; et le clapotis bas de l'eau morte et lourde
Chuchote un gros baiser sous sa carène sourde.
Parmi les yeux du brai flottant qui luit en plaque,
Le ciel miroité semble une immense flaque.

---

* Le *bitors* est un gros fil à voile tordu en double et goudronné.

146

BITOR* THE HUNCHBACK

A poor little cuss as brave as any other,
fourth and last aboard a little cutter . . .
proud of being a sailor and eating without
expense, he was cook, ship's boy, and roustabout;
as that, he counted forty years of service,
always entered on the roll as 'novice'!—

. . . A real hunchback, neck twisted and awry,
in his shell he guarded his worth, for he was sly;
everyone knows at sea a hunchback's good omen . . .
nothing f—— up trouble like a priest or a woman!

His name: it was Bitor—alias of the sea—
he said it was in Chile an earthquake
had ruined him when he was young, well-shaped;
and demolished as well his boat and coconut trees.

. . . .

The sun is drowned.—At evening, in the harbor,
the ship rocks on its cables, in a lull
asleep; the slap of dead and heavy water
whispers a big kiss under the deaf hull.
On the shining eyes of pitch that float around,
the sky reflected seems an immense pond.

---

* The *bitors* is a piece of coarse sail-twine twisted double and
tarred. [Corbière's note.]

Le long des quais déserts où grouillait un chaos
S'étend le calme plat...
                              Quelques vagues échos...
Quelque novice seul, resté mélancolique,
Se chante son pays avec une musique...
De loin en loin, répond le jappement hagard,
Intermittent, d'un chien de bord qui fait le quart,
Oublié sur le pont...
                              Tout le monde est à terre.
Les matelots farauds s'en sont allés — mystère! —
Faire, à grands coups de gueule et de botte... l'amour.
— Doux repos tant sué dans les labeurs du jour. —
Entendez-vous là-bas, dans les culs-de-sac louches,
Roucouler leur chanson ces tourtereaux farouches!...

— Chantez! la vie est courte et drôlement cordée!...
Hâle à toi, si tu peux, une bonne bordée
A jouer de la fille, à jouer du couteau...
Roucoulez, mes Amours! Qui sait: demain!... tantôt...

... Tantôt, tantôt... la ronde, en écrémant la ville,
Vous soulage en douceur quelque traînard tranquille
Pour le coller en vrac, léger échantillon,
Bleu saignant et vainqueur, au clou. — Tradition. —

.   .   .   .

Along the deserted wharves where swarmed a chaos
stretches a dead calm . . .
                              and some vague echoes . . .
some melancholy young shipmite, alone,
is singing the music of his distant home . . .
and now and then a savage yapping's heard
from a ship's dog that stands his watch aboard,
forgotten on the deck . . .
                              all hands are ashore.
Shouting and stamping, the conceited tars
have gone to make—and here's a mystery!—love.
—You have to sweat to earn that sweet repose.—
In the dim alleys you'll hear—listen close—
the cooing of these ferocious turtledoves! . . .

—Sing! so drolly twisted's our short life! . . .
Drag down a leave for yourself—it's worth a try—
for playing with a girl, or with a knife . . .
Coo, lads! Who knows: tomorrow! . . . by and by . . .

. . . By and by . . . the night-patrol, skimming the town,
cools you off neatly: some inoffensive rover,
as a mere sample, like loose cargo is thrown
in the clink, bleeding but cocky.—Happens over and over.—

.   .   .   .

Mais les soirs étaient doux aussi pour le Bitor,
Il était libre aussi, maître et gardien à bord...
Lové tout de son long sur un rond de cordage,
Se sentant somnoler comme un chat... comme un sage,
Se repassant l'oreille avec ses doigts poilus,
Voluptueux, pensif, et n'en pensant pas plus,
Laissant mollir son corps dénoué de paresse,
Son petit œil vairon noyé de morbidesse!...

— Un *loustic* en passant lui caressait les os:
Il riait de son mieux et faisait le gros dos.

.   .   .   .

Tout le monde a pourtant quelque bosse en la tête...
Bitor aussi — c'était de se payer la fête!
Et cela lui prenait, comme un commandement
De Dieu: vers la Noël, et juste une fois l'an.
Ce jour-là, sur la brune, il s'ensauvait à terre
Comme un rat dont on a cacheté le derrière...
— Tiens: Bitor disparu. — C'est son jour de sabbats.
Il en a pour deux nuits: réglé comme un compas.
— C'est un sorcier, pour sûr... —
                                        Aucun n'aurait pu dire,
Même on n'en riait plus; c'était fini de rire.

But the evenings were also sweet for Bitor,
he was free too, master and guard aboard . . .
curled at full length around a coil of cordage,
feeling like a drowsy cat, or sage,
his hairy fingers scratching at his ear,
voluptuous, pensive, nothing very clear,
letting himself relax in idleness,
his little wall-eyes drowned in sluggishness! . . .

—When a passing joker gave his bones a thump,
he would laugh his best and arch his hump.

. . . .

Everyone's got some crotchet, everyone . . .
Bitor too—to have himself some fun!
Like one of God's commandments, he could hear
it toward Christmas, and just once a year.
On that day, in the dusk, he'd escape to land,
wild as a rat with a stoppered-up rear end . . .
—Well, Bitor's disappeared.—Gone on a bat
for two nights: true as a compass. And that's that.
—He's a wiz, for sure . . . —
                            No one knew what to say,
nobody laughed any more; he was just that way.

Au deuxième matin, le *bordailleur* rentrait
Sur ses jambes en pieds-de-banc-de-cabaret,
Louvoyant bord-sur-bord...

                     Morne, vers la cuisine
Il piquait droit, chantant ses vêpres ou matines,
Et jetait en pleurant ses savates au feu...
— Pourquoi — nul ne savait, et lui s'en doutait peu.
... J'y sens je ne sais quoi d'assez mélancolique,
Comme un vague fumet d'holocauste à l'antique...

C'était la fin; plus morne et plus tordu, le hère
Se reprenait hâler son bitor de misère...

   .   .   .   .

— C'est un soir, près Noël. — Le cotre est à bon port,
L'équipage au diable, et Bitor... toujours Bitor.
C'est le grand jour qu'il s'est donné pour prendre terre:
Il fait noir, il est gris. — L'or n'est qu'une chimère!
Il tient, dans un vieux bas de laine, un sac de sous...
Son pantalon à mettre et: — La terre est à nous! —

... Un pantalon jadis *cuisse-de-nymphe-émue,*
Couleur tendre à mourir!... et trop tôt devenue
Merdoie... excepté dans les plis *rose d'amour,*
Gardiens de la couleur, gardiens de pur contour...

The *watchman* always returned on the second day,
on legs that felt like a bench in a cabaret,
tacking from side to side . . .
                            and straight he'd sally,
singing his vespers or matins, to the galley,
gloomy and weeping, to burn his old shoes . . .
—why—no one knew, and for him it was 'just because.'
. . . I smell from it something sad—what, I don't know,—
like a whiff from altar-fires of long ago . . .

That done, more bleak and warped than ever, he
would tan some more his twist of misery . . .

. . . .

—One night, near Christmas, the cutter in port once more,
the crew gone to blazes, and Bitor . . . always Bitor.
It's the big day that he's taking for shore leave:
it's dark, he's drunk.—Money's just makebelieve!
In an old wool sock he takes a sack of coin . . .
his pants to put on and then:—The world is mine!—

Breeches once colored like a *wild nymph's thigh,*
an utterly delicate hue! . . . too easily
dirtied . . . except in the wrinkles *rose d'amour,*
conservators of color, of pure contour . . .

Enfin il s'est lavé, gratté — rude toilette!
— Ah! c'est que ce n'est pas, non plus, tous les jours fête!...
Un cache-nez lilas lui cache les genoux.
— Encore un coup-de-suif! et: La terre est à nous!
... La terre: un bouchon, quoi!... — Mais Bitor se sent riche:
D'argent, comme un bourgeois: d'amour, comme un caniche...
— Pourquoi pas le *Cap-Horn!*... Le sérail — Pourquoi pas!...
— Sirènes du *Cap-Horn,* vous lui tendez les bras!...

. . . . . Ce bagne-lupanar
Qu'ils nomment le *Cap-Horn,* dans leur langue hâlée.

(*Les Matelots,* page 245.)

. . . .

Au fond de la venelle est la lanterne rouge,
Phare du matelot, *Stella maris* du bouge...
— Qui va là? — Ce n'est plus Bitor! c'est un héros,
Un Lauzun qui se frotte aux plus gros numéros!...
C'est Triboulet tordu comme un ver par sa haine!...
Ou c'est Alain Chartier, sous un baiser de reine!...
Lagardère en manteau qui va se redresser!...
— Non: C'est un bienheureux honteux — Laissez passer.
C'est une chair enfin que ce bout de rognure!
Un partageux qui veut son morceau de nature.
C'est une passion qui regarde en dessous
L'amour... pour le voler!... — L'amour à trente sous!

Washed, scrubbed—rude primping!—at last he says:
—Ah, why are all the days not holidays! . . .
A lilac muffler hides his knees.—A shine
with a swipe of tallow! and the world is mine!
. . . The world: a grogshop, huh! . . . —Bitor feels rich:
in money, like a tradesman; in love, like a bitch . . .
—Why not the Cape Horn? . . . The brothel—well, why not! . . .
—Those Cape Horn sirens' arms will hug the lot! . . .

> . . . . . . That prison-brothel
> they call the 'Cape Horn' in their twisted speech.
> *(Les Matelots)*

. . . .

Down the alley the red lantern, whorehouse star,
Star of the Sea, the beacon of the tar . . .
—Who's there?—It's no more Bitor! it's a hero,
a Lauzun who rubs shoulders with no zeros! . . .
It's Triboulet, twisted like a worm with spleen! . . .
Or it's Alain Chartier, kissed by a queen! . . .
Lagardère, in his cloak, who seeks revenge! . . .
—No: a sheepish happy fellow—let him range.
This is only the paring's-end of a creature!
A socialist who wants his share from nature.
A passion that is gazing from below
at love . . . to filch it! . . . love at two bits a throw!

— Va donc, Paillasse! Et le trousse-galant t'emporte!
Tiens: c'est là!... C'est un mur — Heurte encor!... C'est la porte:
As-tu peur! —
         Il écoute... Enfin: un bruit de clefs,
Le judas darde un rais: — Hô, quoi que vous voulez?
— J'ai de l'argent. — Combien es-tu? Voyons ta tête...
Bon. Gare à n'entrer qu'un; la maison est honnête;
Fais voir ton sac un peu?... Tu feras travailler?... —
Et la serrure grince, on vient d'entre-bâiller;
Bitor pique une tête entre l'huys et l'hôtesse,
Comme un chien dépendu qui se rue à la messe.
— Eh, là-bas! l'enragé, quoi que tu veux ici?
Qu'on te f..iche droit, quoi? pas dégoûté! Merci!...
Quoi qui te faut, bosco?... des nymphes, des pucelles?
Hop! à qui le Mayeux — ? Eh là-bas, les donzelles!... —

Bitor lui prit le bras: — Tiens, voici pour toi, gouine:
Cache-moi quelque part... tiens, là... C'est la cuisine.
— Bon. Tu m'en conduiras une... et propre! combien?...
— Tire ton sac. — Voilà. — Parole! il a du bien!...
Pour lors nous en avons du premier brin: *cossuses;*
Mais on ne t'en a pas fait exprès des *bossuses*...
Bah! la nuit tous les chats sont gris. Reste là voir,
Puisque c'est ton caprice; as pas peur, c'est tout noir.

. . . .

—Get along, Clown! And the cold sweat plague you sore!
Well, here it is! . . . It's a wall—Knock again! . . . it's the door:
Are you scared?—
                            He listens . . . finally, the rattle of keys,
a glint from the judas-window:—Hey, who's there?
—I've money.—How many are you? Let's see your face . . .
Good. Just one at a time, now; we're on the square;
let's have a look at your purse? . . . You'll do your chore? . . . —
The lock grates, someone's just half-opened the door;
Bitor pokes his head between jamb and hostess,
like a dog, cut down from hanging, that rushes to Mass.
—What do you want here, crazy? you, short-shanks?
To get f—— proper, and nobody squeamish? Thanks! . . .
What's your meat, hunch? . . . virgins and nymphs, no doubt?
Who gets this Mayeux—? Hey, you, girls, come out! . . . —

Bitor takes her arm:—Fluff, here's for you:
hide me somewhere . . . there . . . —In the kitchen?—That'll do.
Now bring me a . . . and clean! How much? . . . —Show me
your purse.—Here.—You're sure well-heeled! Let's see . . .
we've got some first-rate young stuff, tailor-made;
but we don't cater to hunchbacks in our trade . . .
bah! in the night all cats are gray. Wait here,
since that's your whim; it's dark enough, no fear.

.   .   .   .

Une porte s'ouvrit. C'est la salle allumée.
Silhouettes grouillant à travers la fumée:
Les amateurs beuglant, ronflant, trinquant, rendus;
— Des Anglais, jouissant comme de vrais pendus,
Se cuvent, pleins de stout et de béatitude;
— Des Yankees longs, et roide-soûls par habitude,
Assis en deux, et tour à tour tirant au mur
Leur jet de jus de chique, au but, et toujours sûr;
— Des Hollandais salés, lardés de couperose;
— De blonds Norvégiens, hercules de chlorose;
— Des Espagnols avec leurs figures en os;
— Des baleiniers huileux comme des cachalots;
— D'honnêtes caboteurs bien carrés d'envergures,
Calfatés de goudron sur toutes les coutures;
— Des Nègres blancs, avec des mulâtres lippus;
— Des Chinois, le chignon roulé sous un *gibus,*
Vêtus d'un frac flambant neuf et d'un parapluie;
— Des chauffeurs venus là pour essuyer leur suie;
— Des Allemands chantant l'amour en orphéon,
Leur patrie et leur chope... avec accordéon;
— Un noble Italien, jouant avec un mousse
Qui roule deux gros yeux sous sa tignasse rousse;
— Des Grecs plats; des Bretons à tête biscornue;
— L'escouade d'un vaisseau russe, en grande tenue;
— Des Gascons adorés pour leur galant bagout...
Et quelques renégats — écume du ragoût. —

A door is opened. It's a lighted room.
Silhouettes swarming in the smoky fumes:
customers bawling, clinking, snoring—all-in;
—some English, enjoying themselves like real hanged men,
are sleeping it off, full of stout and beatitude;
—tall Yankees, and stiff-drunk by habitude,
seated by twos and shooting tobacco-spit
at a target on the wall, and always a hit;
—some dirty Dutchmen, fat, with blotchy faces;
—blond Norwegians, greensick Herculeses;
—cadaverous Spaniards, a lean and bony lot;
—whalers as oily as their cachalots;
—some honest coasters, big, square in the beam,
and caulked with tar in all their clothing's seams;
—white Negroes, and blubber-lipped mulattoes;
—Chinese, with queues stuffed in their opera-hats,
with umbrellas and brand-new frock coats;
—stokers come here to wipe off their soot;
—Germans with an accordion, a male choir,
singing of love, the Fatherland, and beer;
—a noble Italian, caressing a cabin-boy
who under his red mop rolls two big eyes;
—some stupid Greeks; Bretons with monstrous heads;
—a Russian ship's crew, dressed to knock you dead;
—some Gascons, much admired for their blague and dash . . .
and some renegades—the scum of the whole goulash.—

Là, plus loin dans le fond, sur les banquettes grasses,
Des novices légers *s'affalent* sur les Grâces
De corvée... Elles sont d'un gras encourageant;
Ça se paye au tonnage, on en veut pour l'argent...
Et, quand on *largue tout,* il faut que la viande
Tombe, comme un *hunier qui se déferle en bande!*

— On a des petits noms: *Chiourme, Jany-Gratis,*
Bout-dehors, Fond-de-Vase, Anspeck, Garcette-à-ris.
— C'est gréé comme il faut: satin rose et dentelle;
Ils ne trouvent jamais la mariée assez belle...
— Du velours pour frotter à cru leur cuir tanné!
Et du fard, pour torcher leur baiser boucané!...
A leurs ceintures d'or, faut ceinture dorée!
Allons! — *Ciel moutonné, comme femme fardée*
N'a pas longue durée à ces Pachas d'un jour...
— *N'en faut du vin! n'en faut du rouge!... et de l'amour!*

. . . .

There, farther toward the back, on greasy benches,
the dizzy beginners flop down on the wenches,
Graces on duty . . . encouragingly fat;
paid for by tonnage, for their money men like that . . .
and when one *looses out,* flesh must uncurl
like a *tops'l that all at once unfurls!*

—They have their nicknames: *Chain-gang, Jenny Free-mounting,*
Arse-out, Handspike, Reef-point, Muddy-sounding.
—All rigged and shipshape, in pink satin and lace;
they never find bridal garments to their taste . . .
—On their bare tanned skin rub velvet dresses!
Lipstick to freshen up their cured-meat kisses! . . .
For their tawny waists gilt belts are what they want!
Come on!—*Summer sky, like a painted woman, can't*
last much longer for these Pashas of
a day . . . —*Let not wine lack! or rouge! . . . or love!*

.   .   .   .

Bitor regardait ça — comment on fait la joie —
Chauve-souris fixant les albatros en proie...
Son rêve fut secoué par une grosse voix:
— Eh, dis donc, l'oiseau bleu, c'est-y fini ton choix?
— Oui: (ses yeux verts vrillaient la nuit de la cuisine)
... La grosse dame en rose avec sa crinoline!...
— Ça: c'est *Mary-Saloppe*, elle a son plein et dort. —
Lui, dégaînant le bas qui tenait son trésor:
— Je te dis que je veux la belle dame en rose!...
— Ça-t'y du vice!... Ah çà: t'es porté sur la chose?...
Pour avec elle, alors, tu feras dix cocus,
Dix tout frais de ce soir!... Vas-y pour tes écus
Et paye en double: On va t'*amatelotter*. Monte...
— Non, ici... — Dans le noir? allons! faut pas de honte!
— Je veux ici! — Pas mèche, avec les règlements.
— Et moi je veux! — C'est bon... mais t'endors pas dedans...

Bitor watched all this—how people play—
bats spotting albatrosses as their prey . . .
His dream was shaken by a raucous voice:
—Well, speak up, Bluebird, have you made your choice?
—Yes: (his green eyes drill the kitchen's night)
. . . the fat dame in pink crinoline's all right! . . .
—That's *Slutty Mary,* she's had enough and sleeps.—
He pulls out the sock that holds his heap:
—I tell you I want that pretty dame in pink! . . .
—You're a sly fox! . . . You're sure of what you think? . . .
With her, you'll make ten cuckolds; ten times fresh
this evening she's been had! . . . Out with your cash,
pay double: she'll *unsailor* you. Up you go . . .
—No, here . . . —In the dark? Let's not be bashful!—Here,
I say!—Not the ghost of a chance. The rules, you know.
—I want it!—O.K. . . . but don't fall asleep in there . . .

Ohé là-bas! debout au quart, *Mary-Saloppe!*
— Eh, c'est pas moi *de quart!* — C'est pour prendre une chope,
C'est rien *la corvée*... accoste: il y a gras!
— De quoi donc? — Va, c'est un qu'a de l'or plein ses bas,
Un bossu dans un sac, qui veut pas qu'on l'évente.
— Bon: qu'y prenne son soûl, j'ai le mien! j'ai ma pente.
— Va, c'est dans la cuisine...
                                        — Eh! voyons, toi, Bichon,
T'es tortu, mais j'ai pas peur d'un tire-bouchon!
Viens... Si ça t'est égal: éclairons la chandelle?
— Non. — Je voudrais te voir, j'aime Polichinelle...
Ah! je te tiens; on sait jouer Colin-Maillard!...
La matrulle ferma la porte...
                                        — Ah! tortillard!...

. . . .

— Charivari! — Pour qui? — Quelle ronde infernale,
Quel paquet crevé roule en hurlant dans la salle?...
— Ah, peau de cervelas! ah, tu veux du chahut!
A poil! à poil! on va te *caréner* tout cru!
Ah! tu grognes, cochon! Attends, tu veux la goutte:
Tiens son ballon!... Allons, avale-moi ça... toute!
Gare au grappin, il croche! Ah! le cancre qui mord!
C'est le diable bouilli!...
                                        C'était l'heureux Bitor.

Hey, below! Slutty Mary, hit the deck!
—It's not my *watch!*—It's only for a bock,
in line of duty . . . come alongside: he's flush!
—What with?—I tell you his sock's full of cash;
hunchback in a poke, doesn't want to be seen. He's shy.
—Good: I wish him a bellyfull, like mine! But I'll try.
—Go into the kitchen . . .

    —Ducky, let's look at you;
you're crooked, but I'm not afraid of a mere corkscrew!
Come on . . . if you don't mind, shall we make a light?
—No.—Let me see! I always did love Punch . . .
I've got you; we can play Blindman's Buff, all right! . . .
The madam closes the door . . .

    —Ah, little hunch! . . .

. . . .

—Roughhouse!—Who for?—What a hell of a brawl,
what smashed lump rolls howling down the hall? . . .
—Ah, sausage-skin! you looking for a row?
Strip him! We'll *careen* you in the raw!
Ah, pig, you're grunting! Here, you want a drop:
hoist his backsides! . . . Come on, drink this up!
Look out for hooks, he claws! This crab's a biter!
The devil's hard-boiled! . . .

    It was the happy Bitor.

165

— Carognes, criait-il, mollissez!... je régale...
— Carognes?... Ah, roussin! mauvais comme la gale!
Tu régales, Limonadier de la Passion?
On te régalera, va! double ration!
Pou crochard qui montais nous piquer nos *punaises!*
Cancre qui viens manger nos *peaux!*... Pas de foutaises,
Vous autres: Toi, *la mère,* apporte de là-haut,
Un grand tapis de lit, en double et comme-y faut!...
Voilà! —
   Dix bras tendus halent la couverture.
— Le *tortillou* dessus!... On va la danser dure;
Saute, Paillasse! hop là!... —
     C'est que le matelot,
Bon enfant, est très dur quand il est *rigolot.*
Sa colère! c'est bon. — Sa joie: ah, pas de grâce!...
Ces dames rigolaient...
     — Attrape: pile ou face?
Ah, le malin! quel vice! il échoue en côté! —
... Sur sa bosse grêlaient, avec quelle gaîté!
Des bouts de corde en l'air sifflant comme couleuvres;
Les sifflets de gabier, rossignols de manœuvres,
Commandaient et rossignolaient à l'unisson...
— Tiens bon!... —
   Pelotonné, le pauvre hérisson
Volait, rebondissait, roulait. Enfin la plainte
Qu'il rendait comme un cri de poulie est éteinte...
— Tiens bon! il fait exprès... Il est dur, l'entêté!...
C'est un lapin! ça veut le jus plus pimenté:
Attends!... —

—Bitches, he yelled, lay off! It's my party . . . —Bitches?
. . . ah, stool-pigeon, nasty as the itch!
So you're giving a party, Sop-boy of Christ's Passion?
We'll party you! Give him a double ration!
Crooked louse who mount us just to prick
our *bedbugs,* crab who eat our *skin!* . . . No tricks,
you others: You, *Mama,* bring down from upstairs
your biggest bedspread, folded double with care! . . .
So!—
      Ten arms reach to stretch the cover tight.
—Put the *dwarf* in it! . . . A tough dance, all right.
Jump, Clown, hop! there!—
               Ah, this sailor's tough,
good fellow, and has *fun* when things go rough.
He's angry! Good.—He likes it; have no mercy! . . .
These women were amused . . .
                 —Catch: arsy-versy!
Ah, evil one! he's run aground— . . . Like hail
they beat upon his hump. How gay they are!
the rope-ends hissing snakelike through the air;
the topman's whistles, rigging-nightingales,
whistled and gave orders all at once . . .
—Good! . . . —
      The poor sea-urchin flew and bounced,
rolled like a ball. Finally his complaints,
like the shrieks of pulleys, became faint . . .
—Good! He means it . . . He's bull-headed and tough! . . .
This rabbit wants more pepper. That's enough!
Wait! . . . —

Quelques couteaux pleuvent... *Mary-Saloppe*
D'un beau mouvement, hèle: — A moi sa place! — Tope!
Amène tout en vrac! largue!... —
                          Le jouet mort
S'aplatit sur la planche et rebondit encor...

Comme après un doux rêve, il rouvrit son œil louche
Et trouble... Il essuya, dans le coin de sa bouche,
Un peu d'écume avec sa chique en sang... —C'est bien;
C'est fini, matelot... Un coup de *sacré-chien!*
Ça vous remet le cœur; bois!... —
                          Il prit avec peine
Tout l'argent qui restait dans son bas de laine
Et regardant *Mary-Saloppe:* — C'est pour toi,
Pour boire... en souvenir... — Vrai! baise-moi donc, quoi!...
Vous autres, laissez-le, grands lâches! mateluches!
C'est mon amant de cœur... on a ses coqueluches:
... Toi: file à l'embellie, en double, l'asticot:
L'échouage est mauvais, mon pauvre saligot!... —

Son œil marécageux, larme de crocodile,
La regardait encore... — Allons, mon garçon, file! —

.   .   .   .

C'est tout. Le lendemain, et jours suivants, à bord
Il manquait. — Le navire est parti sans Bitor. —

.   .   .   .

              Some knives flash . . . Slutty Mary shouts,
impulsively:—Take me!—Done! Throw this out!
Into the rubbish! Slack it! . . . —
                              The dead toy then
is banged on the floor and bounces once again . . .

As after a sweet dream, opening wet lids,
squinting, he wiped some foam from the bloody quid
at the corner of his mouth . . . —It's not too bad,
sailor, it's over . . . and it's time you had
a hair of the dog, for courage. Drink! . . . —
                                        With pain
he takes what money's left in his sock, and then,
gazing at Slutty Mary:—It's for you,
for a little tip . . . in memory . . . —Is that true?
Then kiss me! . . . You sailors' bitches, let him alone!
He's my sweetheart . . . every girl has some.
. . . You now, get cleaned up, quickly too, my lad:
poor little fish, that running aground was bad! . . . —

With marshy eye and crocodile tears he looks
at her once more . . . —Come, laddy, slip your hooks!—

.   .   .   .

That's all. He was missing on board, day after day.—
Then, without Bitor, the ship sailed away.—

.   .   .   .

Plus tard l'eau soulevait une masse vaseuse
Dans le dock. On trouva des plaques de vareuse...
Un cadavre bossu, ballonné, démasqué
Par les crabes. Et ça fut jeté sur le quai,
Tout comme l'autre soir, sur une couverture.
Restant de crabe, encore il servit de pâture
Au rire du public; et les gamins d'enfants
Jouant au bord de l'eau noire sous le beau temps,
Sur sa bosse tapaient comme sur un tambour
Crevé...
        — Le pauvre corps avait connu l'amour.

(Marseille. — La Joliette. — Mai.)

Later a slimy mass was cast by the water
onto the dock. A sailor's jacket in tatters . . .
a hunchback's carcass, swollen, face gnawed away
by crabs. And that had been tossed on the quay,
just as the other night, on a bedspread.
Left by the crabs, he still served as Turk's-head
for the public's joke. And the gutter-brats, together
playing along the black water, in the nice weather,
beat on his hump, like the cracked parchment of
a drum . . .
       —This wretched body had known love.

              (Marseille.—La Joliette.—May.)

BAMBINE

Tu dors sous les panais, capitaine Bambine
Du remorqueur havrais l'*Aimable-Proserpine,*
Qui, vingt-huit ans, fis voir au Parisien béant,
Pour vingt sous: *L'OCEAN! L'OCEAN!! L'OCEAN!!*

Train de plaisir au large. — On double la jetée —
En rade: *y a-z-un peu d'gomme...* — Une mer démontée —
Et *la cargaison* râle — Ah! commandant! assez!
Assez, pour notre argent, de tempête! cessez! —

Bambine ne dit mot. Un bon coup de mer passe
Sur les infortunés: — Ah, capitaine! grâce!...
— C'est bon... si ces messieurs et dam's ont leur content?...
C'est pas pour mon plaisir, moi, v'sêt's mon chargement:
Pare à virer... —
                    Malheur! le coquin de navire
Donne en grand sur un banc... — Stoppe! Fini de rire...
Et talonne à tout rompre, et roule bord sur bord,
Balayé par la lame: — A la fin, c'est trop fort!...

Et la *cargaison* rend des cris... rend tout! rend l'âme.
Bambine fait les cent pas.
                        Un ange — une femme! —
Le prend: — C'est ennuyeux ça, conducteur! cessez!
Faites-moi mettre à terre, à la fin! — c'est assez! —

BAMBINE

You sleep beneath the parsnips, Captain Bambine
of the Havre tugboat *The Lovable Proserpine,*
who, for twenty-eight years, gave the gaping Parisians a notion,
for twenty sous, of THE OCEAN! THE OCEAN!! THE OCEAN!!

An excursion train afloat.—It doubles the mole—
in the roads: *the fun starts* . . .—there's a hell of a roll—
and *the cargo,* retching, blurts:—Commander, enough!
we've had enough storm for our money! Let us off!

Bambine says not a word. Then an enormous
wave showers them:—Captain, have mercy on us! . . .
—Well . . . if these ladies and gents have enough, all right!
It's not for my pleasure, this trip; you're billed me as freight:
make ready to come about . . . —
                                No luck! this knave
of a tugboat—stop! don't laugh! . . . hurled by a wave,
bumps on a reef, and by each billow tossed
it rolls from side to side:—It's too much! All's lost! . . .

And the *cargo* screams, gives up the ghost already.
Bambine walks the bridge.
                            An angel grabs him—a lady!—
I'm sick of this, conductor! Let me off!
Come on, now, put me ashore!—I've had enough!—

173

Bambine l'élongeant d'un long regard austère:
— A terr'! q'vous avez dit?... vous avez dit: à terre...
A terre! pas dégoûtaî!... Moi-z'aussi, foi d'mat'lot
J'voudrais ben!... attendu qu'si t't-à-l'heure l'prim'flot
Ne soulag' pas la coqu': vous et moi, mes princesses,
J'bérons ben, sauf respect, la lavure éd' nos fesses! —

Il reprit ses cent pas, tout à fait mal bordé:
— A terr'!... j'crâis f..tre ben! Les femm's!... pas dégoûté!

(Havre-de-Grâce, La Hève. — Août.)

Bambine looks her up and down with a hard eye, and:
—Ashore, you said? . . . You said, you'd like to land? . . .
Ashore! You don't want much! . . . I'd like to be
ashore, too, take my word! If the next big sea
doesn't float this shell, my Princesses, off the bumps,
you and I'll drink bilge—no disrespect—up our rumps!—

He goes on walking the bridge, and pretty damn sore:
—Well, I'll be f——d! These women! . . . Not much! Ashore!

(Havre-de-Grâce, La Hève.—August.)

AU VIEUX ROSCOFF

Berceuse en Nord-ouest mineur.

Trou de flibustiers, vieux nid
A corsaire! — dans la tourmente,
Dors ton bon somme de granit
Sur tes caves que le flot hante...

Ronfle à la mer, ronfle à la brise;
Ta corne dans la brume grise,
Ton pied marin dans les brisans...
— Dors: tu peux fermer ton œil borgne
Ouvert sur le large, et qui lorgne
Les Anglais, depuis trois cents ans.

— Dors, vieille coque bien ancrée;
Les margats et les cormorans,
Tes grands poètes d'ouragans,
Viendront chanter à la marée...

— Dors, vieille fille à matelots;
Plus ne te soûleront ces flots
Qui te faisaient une ceinture
Dorée, aux nuits rouges de vin,
De sang, de feu! — Dors... Sur ton sein
L'or ne fondra plus en friture.

— Où sont les noms de tes amants?...
— La mer et la gloire étaient folles! —
Noms de lascars! noms de géants!
Crachés des gueules d'espingoles...

TO OLD ROSCOFF

Lullaby in Northwest minor.

Den of buccaneers, old nest
of corsairs!—in the squall and storm,
in your granite slumber, rest,
above your caverns where tides swarm . . .

Snore with the sea, snore with the breeze;
your horn high in the gray fog-wreaths,
your sea-legs in the rolling seas . . .
—Sleep: you can close your Cyclops' eye,
long open on the main to spy
on the English, these three centuries.

—Sleep, old stoutly anchored hull;
all the cormorants and cranes,
your mighty poets of hurricanes,
will come to sing when the tide runs full . . .

—Sleep, old harlot of the tars;
no more made drunk by those tumbling floods
that used to make for you a belt
of gold, with nights turned red by blood,
by fire, and wine!—No gold will melt
on your breast in the frying.—Sleep!

—Where are now the names of your lovers? . . .
—Sea and glory meant mad carousals!—
Names of giants! names of lascars!
spat from blunderbusses' muzzles . . .

Où battaient-ils, ces pavillons,
Echarpant ton ciel en haillons!...
— Dors au ciel de plomb sur tes dunes...
Dors: plus ne viendront ricocher
Les boulets morts sur ton clocher
Criblé — comme un prunier — de prunes...

— Dors: sous les noires cheminées,
Ecoute rêver tes enfants,
Mousses de quatre-vingt-dix ans,
Epaves des belles années...

.   .   .   .

Il dort ton bon canon de fer,
A plat-ventre aussi dans sa souille,
Grêlé par les lunes d'hiver...
Il dort son lourd sommeil de rouille.
— Va: ronfle au vent, vieux ronfleur,
Tiens toujours ta gueule enragée
Braquée à l'Anglais!... et chargée
De maigre jonc-marin en fleur.

(Roscoff. — Décembre.)

Where did they use to thrash, those flags,
slashing your heavens into rags! . . .
—Sleep under the leaden sky of your dunes . . .
sleep: no more spent cannonballs
will ricochet from the tower of the bells,
riddled—like a prune-tree—with prunes . . .

—Sleep: below black chimneys, hear
all your children as they dream,
cabin-boys of ninety years,
wrecks and waifs of lovely time . . .

. . . .

Your good iron cannon is asleep,
flat-bellied in its bed of dust,
hailed on by the moons of winter . . .
it sleeps a heavy sleep of rust.
—Snore with the wind, old fellow, snore,
your angry muzzle evermore
aimed at the English! . . . and well-loaded
with thin sea-rushes in full flower.

(Roscoff.—December.)

179

LA FIN

Eh bien, tous ces marins — matelots, capitaines,
Dans leur grand Océan à jamais engloutis,
Partis insoucieux pour leurs courses lointaines,
Sont morts — absolument comme ils étaient partis.

Allons! c'est leur métier; ils sont morts dans leurs bottes!
Leur *boujaron* au cœur, tout vifs dans leurs capotes...
— *Morts*... Merci: la *Camarde* a pas le pied marin;
Qu'elle couche avec vous: c'est votre bonne-femme...
— Eux, allons donc: Entiers! enlevés par la lame!
      Ou perdus dans un grain...

Un grain... est-ce la mort, ça? La basse voilure
Battant à travers l'eau! — Ça se dit *encombrer*...
Un coup de mer plombé, puis la haute mâture
Fouettant les flots ras — et ça se dit *sombrer*.

— Sombrer. — Sondez ce mot. Votre *mort* est bien pâle
Et pas grand'chose à bord, sous la lourde rafale...
Pas grand'chose devant le grand sourire amer
Du matelot qui lutte. — Allons donc, de la place! —
Vieux fantôme éventé, la Mort, change de face:
      La Mer!...

THE END

Well, all these seamen—sailors and skippers—they
are swallowed forever in their mighty Sea,
gone off on their distant cruises, quite carefree,
they're dead—as sure as they ever got under way.

What the hell! it's their business! they died in their boots!
grog in their bellies, brisk in their oilskin coats . . .
—*dead* . . . Thanks: old *Snubnose* has no sea-legs at all;
take her to bed with you: she's a brave old pillow . . .
—As for them: they're all gone! hoicked off by a billow!
        or drowned by a sudden squall . . .

A squall . . . is that death? The lower mains'l lashing
over the water!—Well, it's sure a *blunder* . . .
the crash of a leaden sea, then the tall masts thrashing
low on the surge—and that's about where you *founder*.

—Founder.—Probe that word. Your *death* is pale
and no great shakes on board, in a heavy gale . . .
small stuff compared with the bitter irony
of a struggling sailor's grin.—Come, clear a place!—
Old dried-out specter, Death, by change of face:
        the Sea!

Noyés? — Eh allons donc! les *noyés* sont d'eau douce.
— Coulés! corps et biens! Et, jusqu'au petit mousse,
Le défi dans les yeux, dans les dents le juron,
A l'écume crachant une chique râlée,
Buvant sans hauts-de-cœur *la grand'tasse salée.*
     — Comme ils ont bu leur boujaron. —

. . . .

— Pas de fond de six pieds, ni rats de cimetière:
Eux ils vont aux requins! L'âme d'un matelot,
Au lieu de suinter dans vos pommes de terre,
    Respire à chaque flot.

— Voyez à l'horizon se soulever la houle;
    On dirait le ventre amoureux
D'une fille de joie en rut, à moitié soûle...
    Ils sont là! — La houle a du creux. —

— Ecoutez, écoutez la tourmente qui beugle!...
C'est leur anniversaire. — Il revient bien souvent. —
O poète, gardez pour vous vos chants d'aveugle;
— Eux: le *De profundis* que leur corne le vent.

... Qu'ils roulent infinis dans les espaces vierges!...
    Qu'ils roulent verts et nus,
Sans clous et sans sapin, sans couvercle, sans cierges!...
— Laissez-les donc rouler, *terriens* parvenus!

                (A bord. — 11 février.)

Drowned?—Ah, yes! the *drowned* are a freshwater crew.
—Sunk! men and cargo! The little ship's-boy, too,
with defiant eyes, in his teeth the last God-damn-it!
spitting his quid, at the death-rattle, into the foam,
and drinking the *big salt cup*—as they'd drink their rum—
      without having to vomit.—

.   .   .   .

—No six-foot hole of earth, no graveyard rats:
they've gone to feed the sharks! The soul of a sailor
doesn't seep up through your potato plots.
      It breathes from every roller.

—See where at the horizon the surges lift
      their amorous bellies and wallow
like a whore in heat, you might say, and half-squiffed . . .
      the lads are there, in the billow's hollow.—

—Listen! the hurricane bawls down the wind! . . .
It's their anniversary.—It quite often returns.—
O poet, keep to yourself your songs of the blind;
—for them: the *De profundis* from the wind's horns.

. . . Naked and green, in the spacious virginal brine,
      may they swirl to infinity!
without shrouds or candles, without nails or pine! . . .
—*Earth-born* parvenus, let them roll in the sea!

                   (On board.—February 11.)

RONDELS POUR APRES

SONNET POSTHUME

Dors: ce lit est le tien... Tu n'iras plus au nôtre.
— Qui dort dîne. — A tes dents viendra tout seul le foin.
Dors: on t'aimera bien — L'aimé c'est toujours *l'Autre*...
Rêve: La plus aimée est toujours la plus loin...

Dors: on t'appellera beau décrocheur d'étoiles!
Chevaucheur de rayons!... quand il fera bien noir;
Et l'ange du plafond, maigre araignée, au soir,
— Espoir — sur ton front vide ira filer ses toiles.

Museleur de voilette! un baiser sous le voile
T'attend... on ne sait où: ferme les yeux pour voir.
Ris: les premiers honneurs t'attendent sous le poêle.

On cassera ton nez d'un bon coup d'encensoir,
Doux fumet! pour la trogne en fleur, pleine de moelle
D'un sacristain très bien, avec son éteignoir.

POSTHUMOUS SONNET

Sleep: this bed's yours . . . you'll come to ours no more.
—Who sleeps dines.—All you'll chew is hay.
Sleep: you'll be loved—it's the *Other* we always adore . . .
Dream: the best-loved is always the farthest away . . .

Sleep: they'll call you the moonbeam's rough-rider!
the splendid unhooker of stars! . . . when night really gets
black; and the ceiling's angel, the thin spider
—hope—in your empty skull will spin her nets.

Nuzzler through a veil! beneath it a kiss
awaits you . . . close your eyes; but where it is,
who knows? Laugh: under the shroud wait the first honors.

Someone will crack your nose with a biff from a censer,
a pleasant whiff! for the rosy, robust phiz
of an immaculate sacristan, coming with his snuffer.

RONDEL

Il fait noir, enfant, voleur d'étincelles!
Il n'est plus de nuits, il n'est plus de jours;
Dors... en attendant venir toutes celles
Qui disaient: Jamais! qui disaient: Toujours!

Entends-tu leurs pas? Ils ne sont pas lourds:
Oh! les pieds légers! — l'Amour a des ailes...
Il fait noir, enfant, voleur d'étincelles!

Entends-tu leurs voix?... Les caveaux sont sourds.
Dors: il pèse peu, ton faix d'immortelles:
Ils ne viendront pas, tes amis les ours,
Jeter leur pavé sur tes demoiselles:
Il fait noir, enfant, voleur d'étincelles!

RONDEL

It's getting dark, child, robber of sparks!
There are no more nights, there are no more days;
sleep . . . and wait those who will remark:
Never! and those who will say: Always!

Do you hear their steps? Not heavy, nay:
oh, the light feet!—Love, winged like the larks . . .
it's getting dark, child, robber of sparks!

You hear their voice? . . . Graves are deaf and dark.
Sleep: they weigh little, your immortelles:
your friends the bears will not come, not they,
to throw pavingstones at your demoiselles:
it's getting dark, child, robber of sparks!

DO, L'ENFANT DO...

Buona vespre! Dors: Ton bout de cierge,
On l'a posé là, puis on est parti.
Tu n'auras pas peur seul, pauvre petit?...
C'est le chandelier de ton lit d'auberge.

Du fesse-cahier ne crains plus la verge,
Va!... De t'éveiller point n'est si hardi.
Buona sera! Dors: Ton bout de cierge...

Est mort. — Il n'est plus, ici, de concierge:
Seuls, le vent du nord, le vent du midi
Viendront balancer un fil-de-la-Vierge.
Chut! Pour les pieds-plats, ton sol est maudit.
— *Buona notte!* Dors: Ton bout de cierge...

BY-O, BABY, BY-O!

Buona vespre! Sleep: your bit of taper,
someone put it here, then someone is gone.
You won't be afraid by yourself, poor little one? ...
It's the candlestick for your bedside in the tavern.

Fear no more the whip of those scribblers on paper,
go! ... There's no one dares not let you sleep on.
Buona sera! Sleep: your bit of taper ...

is dead.—There is no longer any doorkeeper:
the wind of the north, the wind of the south, alone,
will come to set your gossamer thread aquiver.
Hush! for the dullards, your clay is malediction.
—*Buona notte!* Sleep: your bit of taper ...

MIRLITON

Dors d'amour, méchant ferreur de cigales!
Dans le chiendent qui te couvrira
La cigale aussi pour toi chantera,
Joyeuse, avec ses petites cymbales.

La rosée aura des pleurs matinales;
Et le muguet blanc fait un joli drap...
Dors d'amour, méchant ferreur de cigales!

Pleureuses en troupeaux passeront les rafales...

La Muse camarde ici posera,
Sur ta bouche noire encore elle aura
Ces rimes qui vont aux moelles des pâles...
Dors d'amour, méchant ferreur des cigales.

MIRLITON

In love, sly smith of cicadas, sleep!
Among your twitch-grass covering
the cicada for you too will sing,
joyous, to his small cymbals' beat.

The dew with morning tears will weep;
and the *muguets* make a fine winding-sheet . . .
in love, sly smith of cicadas, sleep!

Weeping in flocks the squalls will sweep . . .

Here Death the Snub-nosed Muse will cling,
still to your black lips she'll bring
the rhymes that make pale folks' marrow creep . . .
in love, sly smith of cicadas, sleep!

PETIT MORT POUR RIRE

Va vite, léger peigneur de comètes!
Les herbes au vent seront tes cheveux;
De ton œil béant jailliront les feux
Follets, prisonniers dans les pauvres têtes...

Les fleurs de tombeau qu'on nomme Amourettes
Foisonneront plein ton rire terreux...
Et les myosotis, ces fleurs d'oubliettes...

Ne fais pas le lourd: cercueils de poètes
Pour les croque-morts sont de simples jeux,
Boîtes à violon qui sonnent le creux...
Ils te croiront mort — Les bourgeois sont bêtes —
Va vite, léger peigneur de comètes!

A LITTLE DEATH TO MAKE ONE LAUGH

Go quickly, nimble comber of comets!
The wind-blown grass will be your poll;
elf-fires will flash from your hollow sockets,
prisoners in the sorry skulls . . .

the flowers of the grave called Amourettes
will swell your earthy laughter full . . .
and forget-me-nots, flowers of oubliettes . . .

Don't make it heavy: coffins for poets
are easy for hired mutes to follow,
fiddle-boxes that sound hollow . . .
they'll think you are dead—the bourgeois are fools—
go quickly, nimble comber of comets!

NOTES

ÇA

Chronologically, the Parisian poems included in this section come later than those in ARMOR and GENS DE MER. Apparently following the admonition of Horace, Corbière has set us down *in medias res*. And he was right in so doing, for the latter part of his book includes the real masterpieces. Verlaine should not for that reason, however, have belittled these poems conceived in Paris. Corbière lets us into his secret immediately, in the poem entitled "Ça?"

Ça? p. 20—

Note that the name of this title poem is followed by a question mark; the intonation is offhand-derogatory. The poet considerately defines by the subtitular quotation. Then he analyzes his work and himself, either as he believes himself to be or as he prefers to have the reader think he is. Denying that "Ça?" is a manifesto, an *ars poetica,* he produces exactly that. But, like the notebooks of Leonardo, the writing must be read in a mirror; for he often says just what he doesn't mean, in his left-handed fashion. The interlocutory method has a long and honorable history, as in the Upanishads, Plato's dialogues, and many of the Body-and-Soul colloquies; it appears today in the patter of the gagman and the stooge. In the present poem, the airy dialogue is often purposely misleading. Just as he is pulling away at the reader's leg, grinning all the while like "angels when they lie," he is telling something he really means. It is a form of confession, like those of St. Augustine, Rousseau, Amiel, or George Moore.

Racine could not have made much of Corbière's French. A modern reader is closer to the Breton than a seventeenth-century compatriot. We have here to do with a modern point of view, with a man who, like Baudelaire, understood good and evil according to our own concepts. We are reading the work of a cocky young fellow who thumbed his nose at the classics and wrote as he pleased. This poem is a map for some pirate's treasure cache; it is barely decipherable, but may lead one to fantastic trove. Line 2 is cer-

tainly true, for—aside from Villon, Baudelaire, and at times, alas, Musset—
he owes little to his predecessors. In stanza 7, perhaps by "du huron, du
Gagne, ou de Musset" he means a gamut of modes, all of them not good:
from the "untutored savage" style (harsh and guttural, though forceful),
through eccentricity (Paulin Gagne's writings were so eccentric as to border
on lunacy: see Larousse, *Dict. du XIXe siècle*), to over-refinement (which
one may suppose would be Corbière's judgment of Musset's poetry). Or it is
possible that "du huron" means in the "noble savage" style *à la* Chateau-
briand. In stanza 9, line 2 indicates Corbière's contempt for the false titles—
"Poems of Passion" with no spark of passion in them, and that sort of
thing—with which the lesser romantics so often labeled their works. If in
the last line of all he chooses to cold-shoulder Art, it is because his pride is
an imp of perversity, that grotesque goblin in a bottle who is as much an
artifact as was Homunculus himself. The subscription of the locale in which
this piece was allegedly written is no doubt mere braggadocio, for I find no
evidence that our poet ever had any serious contretemps with the law. I am
inclined to think it was some red-letter day, perhaps the one on which the
publishers signed the contract. "Now I'm really in for it!" he grins to him-
self, as if he were waiting in court.

Paris nocturne, p. 24—

This and its companion piece were finally published in the *Figaro,* May,
1890—and much good that did Corbière, dead already fifteen years. But the
editor, Ajalbert, seems to have copied the text very carelessly, and I have
been happy to use the readings from Corbière's personal copy, penciled
along the margins, as published by Ida Levi in *French Studies.* Here we
find a subtitular remark for the first poem, different punctuation, and, most
important, in line 18 the word "tête" instead of "terre." This delights me,
for I had long suspected there was a misprint. In the second poem, line 4,
the word "poivré" is a distinct improvement over the *Figaro's* repetition of
"trempé." These two pieces were omitted from the then current editions of
the poems until their absence was remarked by Rémy de Gourmont in his
essay in *Livre des masques,* mentioned above in the Introduction. The noc-
turne is done in five panels, like a broken panorama. Whether the poet was
really reminded of the murmur of the Channel waves by the eternal throb-
bing of the sleeping city, or whether, gazing down from Montmartre
through a night fog, he imagined himself once more on the shores of
Brittany, is anyone's guess. The Diogenes of line 5 is borrowed from Béran-
ger's "Le Nouveau Diogène"; that unexpected phrase, "sans gêne," is in

Béranger's refrain. The ragpickers are a timeless species on which Villon, Baudelaire, and Verlaine had already commented. They are still to be seen, *les chiffoniers,* making their collections from the trash cans put out by the cafés at closing time. Those peripatetic poets, in the same stanza, are really "fishing" in the subconscious. The "sons of Bondy" were traditional robbers from the forest of that name, near Paris. As for the policeman: poets are so often classed as suspicious characters by all the forces of "law and order" that they are hardly to be blamed for returning the compliment; our poet is pleased to have a cop laid out in stanza 4. The prostitute is a sister to those whom Degas and Toulouse-Lautrec will paint in the *maisons closes* where they lived at one time to be near their work. And the charming finale, the dead god under a spray of water on a slab in the Morgue, that, alas, is no longer to be seen. Artificial refrigeration was installed in 1929, and the customers are now kept in a cold-storage room, each in a carefully ticketed drawer which can be pulled out easily for inspection by hopeful relatives, for all the world like a tray for ice cubes.

Paris diurne, p. 26—

I have arbitrarily taken this poem and its predecessor from the "Appendice" to which they have been relegated even as late as in the edition edited by Arnoux, 1947, and have placed them where they belong: as the introduction to the brilliant set of eight sonnets under the general title, "Paris." It is stupid that this has not been done earlier; for here is their proper place. Both of them would be at home in Baudelaire's TABLEAUX PARISIENS, but this one especially is of even tougher quality, with its acerbity and blasphemy. The term "laridons," line 5, comes from La Fontaine's "Oh! combien de Césars deviendront Laridons!" It was a name given to kitchen scullions. The whole spirit of the sonnet is that juvenile rebellion which is not unusual in French poets before they recant and aspire to seats in the Academy or bolt into heaven under the wire. Miss Levi has found in Corbière's personal copy of his book another last line than the one usually given. I follow her lead, for the discovered line is certainly preferable to "Notre substance à nous, c'est notre poche à fiel."

Paris, pp. 28–36—

This octette of slender sonnets—five are included here—is a symbolical biography of the young poet and his Muse, both newly come to Paris in 1872. They lived in a room on the sixth floor, Cité Gaillard, a section, even today, with primitive plumbing and inadequate fire protection. His cousin,

Pol Kalig, writes that Tristan slept habitually on a wooden box and break-fasted at midnight: quite a regime for a sick poet! That is what he told his relative; but two painters, friends of his, maintained that he ate breakfast with them, in regular bourgeois fashion. At any rate, the poet had plunged into the literary maelstrom into which all young writers worth their salt must be swirled. The ensuing poems vibrate as nervously as did earth on creation day, with an electric energy, almost febrile. There is but scant unity of plot in the series, but sometimes the sonnets seem fused by the levin of rage and spleen until they resemble a formation of gravel smitten by lightning and fused into a long, intestinal, snakelike tube of crude glass.

I, p. 28—

The poet introduces himself as a hybrid ("bâtard" implies only that); yet he came, as we have seen, of an above-average family. Leconte de Lisle and Heredia were Creoles, and both Hugo and Baudelaire had mistresses, of café-au-lait color, who were politely so called. The figure of the anthill is used twice by Baudelaire in reference to Paris. The younger poet is acknowl-edging his master. He is right in indicting the climate of Paris, for Roscoff is warmed by the Gulf Stream, and the young man was spoiled. Stanza 2 contains the hurly-burly of a fire, with the old-fashioned bucket brigade in action. Then, after the excitement is over, his virgin Muse stands, proud with the arrogance of all young poets. As a girl newly come to the city, she would be confronted with the eternal question of whether to sell out or not. And the answer the poet postulates later is in the affirmative. "Demoi-selle" in line 10 is an interesting word: it means either a fashionable young lady, a tart, a Numidian crane, or a heavy tamper—what the English call a "beetle"—for work on pavement; the poet was punning, most likely, on "pavement pounder." "Faire le trottoir" has the same meaning. The Muse stands, at the sonnet's end, utterly confused and homesick, as the young poet must have felt when confronted with the literary hubbub of Paris. As a matter of fact, Martineau writes in his biography (p. 71) that Tristan did not frequent the literary cafés and saw few people in Paris except the Count and Marcelle. The landing of his manuscript must have cost some effort, although his father footed the expense: but the book was to come later.

II, p. 30—

The poet considers the potential downfall and decides against it. Lines 3 and 4 are precise description of the life and work of those hack writers who produce strings of "predictable books," each like the last. The career of the venal popular writer is burlesqued in the sestet: the false acclaim, babbled by paid parakeets—reviewers bribed by publishers, or publicity agents who produce a flatulent ecstasy of advertising for public consumption. Naturally, this is "music" to the ears of the author: "Strike up!" The antics of the little gentry of the little magazines are presented in the last line.

V, p. 32—

Whether the gypsy, whoever she may be, is merely a panderess, i.e., the temptation to sell out, or whether she represents some sort of bohemian life, *à la* that of Verlaine and Rimbaud, is not clear. The poet seems to have realized that his youth is gone, so what good the rest of it? Throw it all out but the dregs, the bitter lees of failure. I have never seen a "bamboula" danced, but Webster's dictionary says there is such a thing. Play the game, the final tercet advises, and let your audience, the eternal philistine, take or leave it.

VII, p. 34—

It is typical of Corbière's irony that he should have postulated a failure for his book. "So you think you're in the money! Well, how many others have had a similar illusion and have finally gone off and committed suicide?" "Tramontane" in line 1 has also an idiomatic meaning of "to be at one's wits' end." The poet sees himself as another suffering light-bearer; but he knows that his era—a particularly barren one, by the way—is merely phony painted material. "Monsieur Vautour" is a character exploited by Désaugiers (1772–1827), a writer of *vaudevilles*. The name, of course, means "vulture," and was leveled originally at the type of rapacious landlord who existed before rent controls were established. The truffle stuffage is a fine touch: "elaborately, my boy, as you may have prepared your little masterpiece—those splendidly polished sonnets, those nightingale lyrics,—they're merely to be stuck out for popular consumption." The "four banal" was the communal oven of feudal days, used by lords and vassals alike. The sestet is an allusion to Musset's "Nuit de mai," in which the pelican rends its own flesh to feed its young—with Musset looking on and remarking that thus do poets nourish their readers:

> Pour toute nourriture il apporte son cœur
> . . .
> Poète, c'est ainsi que font les grands poètes.

If Corbière's pelican is a bird employed to catch fish for its owner, his conclusion may represent the humiliation of the young poet who has come to Paris to make a great name for himself, only to subsist on a Grub Street job as a hack whose work catches readers for the editor of a review. If so, the flatness of the last line is appropriate to the bitter hopelessness of the situation.

VIII, p. 36—

The end comes quickly, and here the poet seems to have forgotten about his little girl Muse and to be speaking directly to himself. Liquor—absinthe at that, the downfall of Verlaine—and tuberculosis, which is implied in "ta lèvre écume," are about to kill the poet. Line 4 is a straightforward assertion to which Tristan lived up. You are going to die, the poem continues: prepare your posthumous work (RONDELS POUR APRÈS) for publication. If the artist does not die young, or commit suicide, he may face the worse alternative of lingering after his fame has died. That is the significance of the last two lines: the waiter clears the tablecloth and signifies that he wishes you would go. The "miasmas of glory" which Tristan did not live to breathe came somewhat later, when his book came to be considered one of the cornerstones of Symbolism.

Epitaphe, p. 38—

Here we have a catalogue of paradoxes and antinomies which would have delighted Lao-tze and Chuang-tze. It covers somewhat the same ground as "Ça?" The poet is pleased to imagine himself an enigma—as indeed he was; but he protests too much, and we tire of it. This exhibitionism is quite in the vein of Rousseau, the younger Goethe of *Werther,* and Byron; the pose soon wears thin. The choppy couplets give a translator only slight leeway, for he has to get two rhymes out of eight feet, whereas a quatrain offers more chances for rearrangement and juggling. The first stanza of Villon's "Ballade du Concours de Blois," a poem for which Charles d'Orléans set the first line in one of his competitions among the endless stream of wandering poets he entertained at Blois, gives us at once the source and inspiration for this type of writing in paradox:

> Je meurs de seuf auprès de la fontaine
> Chault comme fue, et tremble dent à dent . . .

LES AMOURS JAUNES

The meaning of this strange title has nowhere been satisfactorily explained. Perhaps if we think of it as implying "jaundiced" or "prematurely autumnal," we shall not be far off. The idiom "rire jaune," which means "to fetch a forced laugh" or "sickly smile," or a "smile from the corner of the mouth," may have been in the author's mind. It certainly connotes some left-handed implication against women, for the section is given over to various ironic situations between the poet and some of the many forms in which he saw, or pretended to see, Marcelle, almost as if she were the old woman of the sea, with powers of metamorphosis. At all events, these various appearances, says Rémy de Gourmont, "are the type of everything else in the world—except 'singularity,' which was the poet's only real love." Considering the intimacy which existed between the two lovers—for her devotion to him in his illness must have involved more than mere friendship,—these are strange poems for a man to write *after* ("après": a word he more than once uses with telling effect).

A l'éternel madame, p. 46—

This is a poem already in the manner of the *symboliste* technique. The keeper of the lupanar, the Venus Pandemos, is an allegory of the venal world, always ready to oblige—at a price—and to corrupt a fresh victim. The setting need not be taken too literally, but there is no doubt about the intended symbolism. Some of my advisers would see in this sonnet the Lady of the Courts of Love, rudely invited down from her pedestal by the worldly modern poet. (Léon Vanier, in his preface to the edition of 1891, p. v, writes that *"L'éternel madame* is a very pretty word from the Courts of Love of the Middle Ages.") But surely so idealistic an interpretation is abnegated by the import clearly shown in the next and companion sonnet! No, she is truly the "eternal feminine," opponent in the duel. As Nietzsche said: "Woman is for danger and for play!" In line 1, the "Turk's-head," as a figure of speech, comes from the good old days when a real specimen used to be exhibited on a pike's point in the market place for the public to throw stones at or otherwise abuse. It was a sort of whipping boy on which to work off the emotions of the populace. In line 9, "en rut"—to which one must add the connotation of a female deer to explain "brame" in line 13, the belling of a male deer in the mating season—becomes less vulgar if the poet's complete picture is considered. Both these terms are used in the cant of venery. *Ame* and *flamme* are often-repeated rhymes in Lamartine, whose name suggests *lame* for the third. And compare, in Hugo's poem "Les Djinns": "Elle brame / Comme une âme / Qu'une flamme / Toujours suit." The last line of Corbière's poem might have been Nietzsche's: "Man's pleasure is *I* will; woman's pleasure is *he* wills." The snoring Conqueror is probably a very realistic touch. But how greedy the poet is, and how unreasonable! He expects the woman to be more than the ideal of the Hindus, viz., "a fountain to man's infancy, a pillow for his prime, a nurse for his old age."

Féminin singulier, p. 48—

A companion piece to the foregoing sonnet. Jocrisse was a stock character in old French comedy: the blockhead, the ninny; "Noddy" is quite accurate for him. As for that *pompier* in line 4, the Parisian fireman is a stern-souled guardian of property; it is difficult to believe that a man in so trusted a civic position would even for a single moment forget his duty. Line 6 reads, literally, "crown ... our heads with ten horns"; this implies cuckoldry in decimal proportions. Remember the cuckoo of Elizabethan drama.

Bonne fortune et fortune, p. 50—

A colloquial confession of defeat. The incident did not necessarily occur in actuality; perhaps Tristan wanted to carry on the situation of Baudelaire's "A une passante" to a more definite conclusion. He often laments his ugliness, but several photographs in the various editions and biographies, scarcely substantiate this complex. In one he looks ethereal, almost Shelley-like, and in another he seems a dapper and elegant young man. His own drawings are always exaggerations—as, in fact, are most of his poems. Returning to this one, we perceive its humorous, burlesque intent. The prowling male is universal, as is the stall he makes about looking for something else besides the girl. This woman knows the answer, and her poise would quash any street flirtation. For "frôler" there seems no exact English equivalent; but from the poet's mention of a "valet de bourreau" one is reminded of the little liberties the executioner's assistant used to take with those ladies who were being readied for the guillotine, under the Terror. Parasols are always cropping out in the poems and paintings of Corbière's day. Remember Seurat's charming pointillistic scene of several couples walking in full sunlight, "Un dimanche d'été à la Grande Jatte," at the Chicago Institute of Art? Laforgue, who used parasols in his verses, also dutifully wrote a poem about the Rue des Martyrs. When I walked along it lately, the drab exteriors and total lack of such women as we find in the poem left me saddened. How the neighborhood has run down in seventy years!

À une camarade, p. 52—

Here is another of those oddly punctuated dialogues between the poet and a woman. It has all been said before, by Catullus: "deprecor illam / assidue; verum disperam nisi amo" (I curse her continually, but may I die if I don't love her!); but it has never been written in such strange tropes as the shedding lizard, the bum of Naples, the cracked trinket, and the final stanza. Line 11, cf. *Le Négrier,* p. 95: "La terre a bien ses brigands, ses contrabandiers, ses Lazzaroni, avec leurs aventures romanesques et quelquefois héroïques." Line 12 has a pun in the French: "breakfasting on fasting." The hunting idiom in stanza 8 means that love has given up and cries "Enough!"

Un jeune qui s'en va, p. 56—

As early as 1827, Goethe had complained to Eckermann of the sickbed romanticists: "All these poets write as if they were ill, and as if the whole world were a hospital. . . . I am going to call their poetry 'hospital poetry' (*Lazareth-Poesie*)." The products of the Consumptive School were too much given to exhibitionistic self-pity. How startlingly different is Tristan's poem, wryly honest, satirical, and dramatic. It could be dramatized; but the effect on an audience would not be the flutter of damp handkerchiefs that is *Camille*'s reward: the beholders would smile at times in spite of themselves, and at times would be politely attentive though puzzled by some of the allusions, and at the end would file out in a silence which would itself be applause. The death-roll of poets, beginning at stanza 15, is a strangely mixed lot. For Murger, for Musset—whose name is of course called as "Rolla," though the "poet of youth" was not taken into the Academy until some twenty years after he had written that early success,—and for Lamartine, Corbière has no sympathies; but it seems gratuitous that he includes Baudelaire with them, considering how much he owes him: perhaps it is only because Baudelaire, too, died early of wrecked health. "Harmonieux" is a word to be found more than once in Lamartine's verse, and so is some form of the verb "moissoner"; the "larme écrite" is from his prose romance, *Graziella.* Hégésippe Moreau (1810–1838), wasted by starvation, entered a hospital and slept in beds used by cholera patients, but ironically was spared at that time the death he sought; he died in the same hospital a few years later when again in Paris. Victor Escousse (1813–1832) at eighteen won acclaim with his verse drama *Farouk le Maure;* but his second play was received with indifference; and on the failure of the third, he and his friend and collaborator Auguste Lebras committed suicide—an event which drew from Béranger a poem entitled "Le Suicide." Escousse and Lebras were looked upon as examples of "ill-fated genius." Gilbert (1751–1780) was a satirist and rebel, bitter in his attacks on those who did not hail his youthful talents. He died of a fall from his horse when out riding. Lacenaire (1800–1836) was a scapegrace whose career of crime ended on the scaffold, whereupon his supposed memoirs and poems— it seems uncertain that he wrote them—had quite a sale; thus Samson, the public executioner, was in a sense his "publisher." Gautier wrote a poem about Lacenaire, in *Emaux et camées,* and called him "real murderer and false poet." Corbière lets Byron off easy, apparently because he suffered physically and yet could summon a mocking laugh. Hugo is called "The man of 'This will kill that' " from the churchman's remark in *Notre-Dame de Paris* (bk. v, chap. i) that the printed book would put an end to the authority of religion. The next stanza is a reminder that the bones of poets dying in poverty get no consideration even in the potter's field. By the change of a single letter the commonplace "J'en ai vu mourir" ("I've seen them die") becomes "J'en ai lu mourir" ("I've *read* them die"), a twist of language characteristic of Corbière. Some editions nevertheless read "vu." Chénier, of course, is the poet of the Revolution who lost his head under the guillotine—and now sings his way through an opera that stops just short of the scaffold. In the penultimate stanza Corbière shows his concern for his work as a poet.

Rousselot (*Tristan Corbière,* pp. 48–49): "We find, at any rate, many proofs that from this sick man and his sick art a new poetry is born, that liquidates the romantic myth *à la française.* . . . Corbiére . . . has made himself quite clear on his refusal to play at 'sensitive souls'; he has only sarcasms for Murger, Musset, Lamartine . . . " The poem is characteristic of several in which Corbière attacked his romantic predecessors.

Le Poète contumace, p. 66—

Arnoux (in his preface to *Les Amours jaunes,* pp. 22–23) affords the following: "The irony of Heine is more affected, has more of artifice and more vaporous Germanism (sentimentality). The *dandysme* of Musset turns pale and evaporates before this harsh sensuality, this rebellious jolting, and these dolorous hiccups, ... this frenetic imprecation. Did such a Marcelle really exist, outside of these stormy nights of caresses? The essence of his solitary vigils, the product of a strong and distracted imagination—did she exist, a subtle, wicked, and voluptuous thing of the flesh?" He concludes that she is largely a poetic pretext around which the poet grouped his work. But there is no doubt that Tristan really suffered about the affair, even if it was purely an imaginary thing. There is some evidence that she had her generous and kindly moments toward the adorer, and I cannot believe that his worship, even though it was a literary affectation, went unrewarded.

As for this particular poem: had Childe Harold, Childe Roland, or any other leading man of romantic poetry, ever happened on such a stage setting, he would have moved right in and felt at home. From romantic drama, one character's voice is actually heard: "Belles nuits pour l'orgie à la tour" pluralizes the opening remark of Orsini the innkeeper as the curtain rises on Act I, scene ii, of Dumas's *Tour de Nesle:* "What a perfect night for an orgy at the tower! The sky is black, the rain is falling, the city sleeps, the river is rising as if to meet corpses ... A wonderful night for love: outside, the roar of thunder; within, the clink of glasses, and kisses, and lovers' murmurings ... " Corbière mentions the Tour de Nesle by name in another poem, "Gente Dame," not included in these translations. In the present poem, the very next line unexpectedly echoes Lamartine, whom the poet has earlier spoken of contemptuously. Corbière: "Nuits à la Roméo!—Jamais il ne fait jour." Lamartine (in the poem "Novissima verba"):

notre cœur enchanté
Dit comme Roméo: «Non, ce n'est pas l'aurore!
Aimons toujours: l'oiseau ne chante pas encore!»

But Tristan's bird, like the nightingale in Boccaccio's story, would have been singing all night long.

At any rate, here the wandering poet settles, hunting a place to die, with his spaniel Tristan II, and Ennui (that faithful Achates of Baudelaire and Mallarmé), the ghost of a lost love, and a covey of careless owls; not to mention his jocular notion of a lease—a notion prompted by the two stanzas of "Le Grand Testament" (lines 990–998) in which Villon "transfers" to Jean Cornu the "garden" (prison, that is)

Que maître Pierre Bobignon
M'arenta, en faisant refaire
L'huis et redresser le pignon.

Corbière had an ironic genius—there is no other word for it—which saved all this. He writes down the hermit poet's story in an imaginary letter to the lost one; then he tears it up (after carefully preserving copies) and gives it to the winds. It is no pale Epipsychidion who inhabits this tower. Corbière's humor, and the very irony with which his self-pity is tempered, produce another fine poem.

Right at the start, in the first introductory stanza, he engages our interest and amuses us. A deserted convent—hmm! But then *voilà!* come those darling donkeys, nibbling away at the shabby ivy on the tower wall, or the turret has a roof like a peaked hat knocked down over one ear! How well he understands these Bretons!—the gossips, the mayor, and the curé all come briefly alive. The hurdy-gurdy and the spaniel, the fields of golden broom, the Armorican heather, the periwinkle dying on a wall, the old poacher who comes at night to sit by the fire—all these sudden pictures make the thing vivid and viable. Corbière has been reading Bernardin de Saint-Pierre and Defoe; he remembers all the right people.

Castagnoles may be the fish called pomfrets (*Brama raii*), which skip vigorously when stranded on a beach; or wooden billets of the kind used to tighten awning-ropes on a vessel. Inès de la Sierra requires some documentation. Her story is from Gautier's poem "Inès de las Sierras" in *Emaux et camées* (1852), which derives from Charles Nodier's romantic novel *Inès de Las Sierras* (1837). Three French officers in Spain come to an old, deserted house: "un vrai château d'Anne Radcliffe" (with some bats by Goya). While they are at supper a vision appears: a woman dancing in black-and-white ribbons; her robe is dank from the tomb and straw-flecked; a faded yellow rose sheds its petals in her black hair, and a fine great wound makes a vermilion gash on her breast. That's enough to show why Inès was used in the poem at hand. Piously Corbière adds a trio of saints: Hubert, Anthony, and Thomas. "Sister Anne," watching from the tower for signs of approaching help, is from Perrault's telling of the Bluebeard story. The "chaumière" in the penultimate stanza is from Bernardin de Saint-Pierre's *La Chaumière indienne,* most likely; at any rate, from one of the Back to Nature idyls so dear to French sentimental romanticism. Although the poet complains of bad weather, he is doing all right when he can pick a batch of mushrooms on his cellar stairs, have plenty of broom for fragrance and color, and a fire of heather, briar, and driftwood. But he is really sad, as the sixth line from the end confesses—the line paralleled by Verlaine in "Ariettes oubliées," III, which begins: "Il pleure dans mon cœur / Comme il pleut sur la ville."

The image of the pieces of torn letter vanishing in the fog is an ideal conclusion. But Tristan's subscribed note, as if he had written the poem at Penmarc'h, at Christmas time, must be looked into. After poking around this district two days, futilely looking for such a place, I conclude that Tristan imagined even the tower. Nor could I find any such cliffs. Le Dantec states, in a note to his 1942 edition of the poems (Vol. I, p. 186): "Although dated at Penmarc'h, this magnificent poem was, in reality, written at Morlaix on the Christmas of 1871. Marcelle had left Roscoff for Paris." He refers also to Martineau's biography, which says (pp. 65–66): "Open the romance of *Tristan et Yseut* (édition Joseph Bédier), to the final pages of the last chapter, and you will find: 'Tristan languished. He yearned for the coming of Yseut. Nothing could comfort him any more, and if he kept on living, it was because he awaited her. Every day, he returned to the shore, to watch for the arrival of the ship and to see the color of its sail. No other desire any longer kept up his heart. Finally he had himself carried to the cliff of Penmarc'h, ... and while the sun was still above the horizon, he gazed far away to sea ...' " And here let us conclude this section with the poet—in his imagination—yearning beside his legendary brother for his own Yseut.

SERENADE DES SERENADES

Under this cocky title are gathered flippant, fugitive pieces: butterflies, night moths, and a few hornets. Many of them remind one of Whistler's signature. Rousselot (*Tristan Corbière*, p. 56): " ... in short verses, dancing, scanned by the guitar, one might say, but also with supplications, groans, womanish humiliations ... and a bit of Satanism, rather cheap (he has read *Les Fleurs du Mal*)." Two of them should suffice.

Guitare, p. 84—

This is almost in the style of a popular song, but it is being strummed by an earlier Segovia, although he pretends to be as tough as Yukon Jake, the Hermit of Shark-tooth Shoal, who "rebetrayed the ruined maid" in the ballad. The one sincere line in the poem may well be "Je suis si laid!"— though he borrows it from Béranger's "Qu'elle est jolie!" the refrain of which is:

> Grands dieux! combien elle est jolie!
> Et moi, je suis, je suis si laid!

But the gamin-like flippancy of the whole is amusing. A poet is under no obligation to mean everything he says. One finds, throughout, a wealth of literary analogies, and numerous quips and quirks. "Amourette" is in Roget's thesaurus: it means a very slight, almost negligible amour. One can see him deftly rolling a cigarette, snapping his fingers, maybe even doing a few braggadocios before a mirror. Let him amuse himself; for aside from his love of Brittany, the sea, and his own art, he had little enough to be happy about. Little Jesus in his manger-crib is very sweet, especially when used here as a symbol of innocence.

Chanson en si, p. 86—

This is another of the poet's puns: the *si* means both the musical note and the conjunction "if." It is this which leads him into an endless string of postulates that might as well have gone on for pages. The form here has gone to pot. His refrains are mostly in the conditional present tense, and that gives him ten easy rhymes—I had to fight for mine. It needs little explanation, except for "Colombelle" (also to be found in La Fontaine), who probably derives from the endearing diminutive, "my little Dove," and not from the gastropod of tropical seas. The melody of these verses is something like that of Swinburne's "A Match": "If love were what the rose is / and I were like the leaf . . . If you were April's lady / And I were lord in May."

RACCROCS

Le Goffic, in his edition of the poems, includes this section as belonging to the *exotiques,* with the preceding group. Martineau, in his biography (p. 90), maintains that the new forms brought in by Corbière helped to renew the worn-out poetry of Romanticism, and even added something to the heritage of Baudelaire by virtue of Tristan's "rude and vigorous Breton nature." And he mentions Raccrocs. The title means "Lucky Hits." Some of the pieces were written when Corbière was in Italy, where Naples and its vicinity seem to have stimulated him greatly.

A ma jument souris, p. 92—

This amusing title turns out to be completely misleading. The French have always loved equitation, horseraces, and steeplechases, and the present piece offers an almost complete description of . . . the sport. Apparently the mount here addressed is a fine filly. She snorts fire, has a wind-blown mane and lots of tail, eyes like burning coals, and a breath perfumed with clover hay. And he is a brave horseman, this jockey, because the leaps entailed in the steeplechase would seem to demand a centaur-like unity of man and mount. The poem should be read aloud to the accompaniment of Haydn's "Horseman's Quartette," for the rhythms of both are a sort of easy lope which at the climax works into a mad gallop.

Frère et sœur jumeaux, p. 94—

A bit different from "Grow old along with me!" and "Silver threads among the gold." The shepherd Tityrus was a symbol of lucky escape from trouble; he comes from the first Eclogue of Vergil, and reappears in Propertius and Edmund Spenser. But it is certainly, as the poet well knew, an off-key note here. A little Latin, in this case, was a dangerous thing. In the "Appendice" of Le Goffic's edition, 1926, there appears a shorter version, omitting stanzas 2, 5, and 7: an example of Corbière's careful ·revision, no matter how careless he pretended to be.

Le Convoi du pauvre, p. 98—

Corbière's book as edited by Arnoux, 1947, was illustrated with vignettes by Patrick de Manceau, and his endpiece to this poem is a rear view of the conventional hearse, with plumes. On the other hand, the edition of Le Dantec, 1942, was illustrated by André Deslignères, and his sketch for the poem shows a humped figure pulling a handcart which carries nothing but a large framed picture. This was the real tip-off. Tristan is not dealing with a pauper's funeral, but in mock-pathetic style with some artist who is hauling his picture away from an exhibition because it has been refused by the jury—"skimmed," as he says, "by the Salon," and perforce retreating from the Grand-Palais des Champs Elysées, where the annual Salons are held, to Montmartre, the artists' Bohemia. The going is hard, and the artist appeals for help like a smart street-gamin: "Give us a push, Mister?" The Rue Notre-Dame-de-Lorette is a street running toward Montmartre; it is called after the early nineteenth-century church, which took its name from the shrine in Italy. Nestor Roqueplan, famous for his *bons mots,* gave the appellation "lorettes" to the demi-mondaines of the district, and Gavarni, whose monument is only a few blocks from the church, drew memorable sketches of them. In stanza 2, the italicized *Cayenne* is not, of course, the penal colony, but may mean "any distant place"; or perhaps it is the name of a bar at which the artist and his friend will recover from their exertions. In stanza 5, the "stations," where they halt for rest, may have sidelong reference to the Stations of the Cross; the artist has already exclaimed, when appealing for help in stanza 1, that his progress is a Via Dolorosa. Stanza 6 goes off in pure parable: the hill is suddenly the difficulty of the artist's life, the ascent of Parnassus. If we do finally get our wings, he says, and think for a moment we are Pegasuses,—the next thing we know, we are just hard-working cart horses, sweating as I am now. The final reference to Courbet may be a slighting one; that capital "P" of "Painter" looks ironical. I can find no significance for the subtitular date. Maybe it was actually the day on which Tristan's picture had been rejected; but it is preposterous to suppose that a young man of his finances should actually pull his handbarrow up that hill.

Déjeuner de soleil, p. 102—

What shall be said of this cheerful song for May Day, so different from Herrick's? What shall be said, except that it is done in the same high spirits as Verlaine's "C'est le chien de Jean de Nivelle" and "Chevaux de bois," those two charming farces in *Romances sans paroles,* which appeared the next year after Corbière's book? The famous "Les lauriers sont coupés" is Banville's, used in English by Housman in "We'll to the woods no more, / The laurels all are cut." The "parsley" may have a bawdy implication; it certainly does in English. The "Serpolet" ("Wild Thyme"), which I couldn't find, was probably a restaurant where it was *comme il faut* to be seen for May Day breakfast. I have asked all the oldest guardians and waiters in the Bois about it, but no one knew the name. In stanza 5, the fragments of conversation seem to indicate a successful and boasting speculator, a gambler, a Dodolphe with his Bébé, and a lady on familiar terms with the sporting aristocracy; or the boisterous voice may be that of an American who has sold his cotton and come to Paris for a holiday, where he is soon picked off by a "babe" who will call him a "duke" or anything else for a cut in those hundred louis! Old "Belle-Impure" of stanza 7 may well have been some elderly demi-mondaine noted for her greediness. The Arthur of stanza 10 is one of those Arthurs and Adolphes (Charlies or Johnnies, we would say; stage-door Johnnies are always with us, and the Champagne Charlie our fathers sang of has many descendants), escorts of opera girls, natural contributors to the gay life of any metropolis. How modern this Arthur seems, with open sport-shirt! And the romanticism affected by the young man about town has led him to name his horse "Byron"! The Diana of the next stanza is one of those stunning horse-women who ride regally in the Bois, more for admiration and applause than for exercise. The Tiger is her smartly liveried young manservant acting as a groom (same sense as in English slang of the period), and the Lions are ageing men of pleasure, well turned out and well mounted, familiar figures of sporting society: see the drawings by Constantin Guys and Toulouse-Lautrec. The *Lettres parisiennes,* 1843, of Delphine Gay (Mme de Girardin) warn against confusing the dandy with the lion: the dandy is "he who wants to be observed," and the lion, "he whom one wants to observe." There is an autumnal pleasure in seeing an old rake, spruce and straight-backed in the saddle, sweep masterfully by. As for the *double entendre* at the end of the poem, *saillent de l'avant:* the poet's listener, presumably a woman, takes him to say that the rider and her mount protrude in front, "All bust and chest," and that, she remarks, is hardly a polite observation. "Beg pardon," he returns, "I'm using a nautical term, 'They're making good headway—sweeping along under full sail,' which describes them handsomely." *Saillent* may be third person plural of either of two verbs, *saillir* or *sailler.*

A l'Etna, p. 106—

The quotation below the title is from the fourth Eclogue and "foreshadows the *Aeneid,*" Professor Fred Carey writes me, and he was kind enough to let my translation stand: "Sicilian Muses, let us now sing somewhat more nobly." Gazing at the mountain beloved by Vergil, Tristan sticks his tongue in his cheek and writes a naughty poem—"more nobly," my eye! Etna is not visible from Palermo, where the piece was written. Stanza 3 outdoes even Baudelaire's morbidity, and it is in bad taste, to shock the bourgeois. It is a question of misery's loving company and engaging in a strange geographic form of "earth-worship," as Norman Douglas discreetly called it. If it weren't for the genders, the last stanza might be perversely suggestive. In line 9, "rire jaune," to "laugh yellow," is to laugh wryly: the volcano rumbles, and gives off yellow sulphurous smoke.

Hidalgo! p. 108—

This lively sketch is in the comic spirit of Daumier's picture of Don Quixote and Sancho Panza. Goya would have loved the scene with those vivid strokes of suspended animation: the horse nibbling the almsman's neck, and the beggar searching with his foot the traveler's pocket. In line 1, the "fiers comme poux sur la gale" is a homely saying, who knows how old? It was used in the dialogue of the *Comédie des proverbes* (1636). In line 2, Corbière underscored *font* to make a light-fingered word of it; "pack your trunk" becomes "unpack" it—filch your valuables; these people are a race of noble pickpockets. Line 5: "suant la race"—their Spanishness fairly oozes out of them. Line 8: since Carnival time, just before Lent, is short, a whole *summer* of Carnival means that this beggar on horseback would do for a protracted season of playing the Cid's part—in a low style, that is, riding around and begging until at last winter should drive him off the road.

ARMOR

The title of this part is the Breton name for Armorica, which is now called Bretagne (Brittany). It is typical of the poet that in the last piece he included in the preceding section, a poem entitled "Paria" not included in these translations, he should make a gesture of emphatic negation that any place meant anything to him—and then put his poems about his homeland right after it. But that valedictory piece was probably done somewhat later than these. The present section would, almost alone, have established him as a major French poet; for he has presented a whole province here, accurately and tenderly, and without pouring in the usual obfuscating mélange of the other parts of the work. It has been cast all of a piece, like a great bell of true metal. Later on, I shall come to my own remarks on the land which was once called Lyonesse, now Léon. But here I want to quote from Le Goffic's preface to *Les Amours jaunes,* 1926 (pp. xxii–xxiii): "[Brittany is a] poor, flat country, bristling with calvaries, without trees, without harvests, a land of professional ship-wreckers and kelp-burners, of moors shriveled by the winds of the sea, of cirques of pale sand strewn like the dust of bones, and of rocks at pasture among the dunes like herds of mammoths." His eloquence reminds me of that in Synge's *Aran Islands.*

Paysage mauvais, p. 112—

This is a fine literary ancestor for many of the Surrealist painters' bone-strewn beaches. Knells are usually rung, not gasped; but "glas" is a word which a Frenchman finds no trouble in associating with that guttural harshness, almost a hoarse breathing, of which bells are capable—especially if they are cracked, as in Gautier's poem "La Vie dans la mort":

> Et, me suivant partout, mille cloches fêlées,
> Comme des voix de mort, me jetaient par volées
> Les râlements du glas.

Corbière connects "glas" with "râle," the death rattle, a gasping cough, in sympathy with his own consumptive paroxysms. "Bruit sur bruit" intensifies the repetition of the rattle and suck of waves on the pebbly beach; but "bruit," being in French a word-of-all-work for any sort of noise, is hardly translatable. What the moon is doing with the worms, who knows? Perhaps worm-shapes of mist, as they pass over the moon's face, seem to be swallowed up. At any rate, worms are appropriate inhabitants of this grim and eerie scene, along with the sorcerer-hare and the toads. The "follet damné" sounds like Hamlet's "goblin damned," but probably this "follet" is a "feu follet," the wandering marsh-light of that maliciously tricksy spirit who lures the curious wanderer to his doom. "Soleil des loups" in line II is a fine idiom for moonlight. Line 14: the Bretons call mushrooms "les trônes des crapauds," a nobler designation than our homely "toadstools." Line 9: Concerning these nocturnal laundresses, Souvestre (*Le Foyer breton,* pp. 115–122) has a tale. A young, unregenerate rascal is going home late at night when he meets an *Ankou*—Breton for the Phantom of Death—dressed like a coachman and driving the dead-wagon drawn by six black horses. The *Ankou* announces that he is searching for the hero, but drives on, apparently unaware that he is speaking to the intended victim. Then the young fellow comes upon laundresses washing beside a hedge of plum trees and hanging the clothes on the bushes to dry. "What are you doing so late in the meadow, little doves?" he asks cheerfully. "We wash, we dry, we mend!" they answer. "But what?" "The shroud of the dead man who still walks and talks." "A dead man! Please tell me his name." When they speak *his* name, he begins to laugh and fearlessly approaches them. They continue to beat their linen while they sing, in the Breton tongue:

> Quen na zui kristen salver
> Rede goëlc'hi hou liçer
> Didan an earc'h ag en aër.

> (Unless some Christian comes to save us,
> we must bleach our linen
> in the snow and the wind.)

Then they beg him to wring the clothes, and he begins helpfully. He recognizes among other laundresses his wife and aunt, his mother and sisters. They are shaking their thin locks, waving their white beaters, and crying, "A thousand sorrows burn our breasts in hell! A thousand sorrows!" Suddenly the shroud catches his arms, like a vice, and he is crushed in the "iron arms of the laundresses."

Nature morte, p. 114—

This little "still-life" sketch is almost as musical as some of Verlaine's wordless melodies; it cuckoos and hoots and goes cawing along so cheerfully that one forgets there's a cadaver to be disposed of. But that is Tristan's *métier,* the final shock. The "brouette de la Mort" is the two-wheeled cart in which the *Ankou* (personification of Death) conveys his nocturnal collections. Sometimes he is said to pull it himself, and sometimes the stories say it is drawn by skeletons or by ghostly horses. Its axles want grease; hence the "cri de bois."

La Rapsode foraine, p. 116—

Anatole Le Braz (*Au pays des pardons,* pp. 249–285) gives a fine account of the Pardon. A local legend has it that Saint Anne was a Bretonne who went to Judea and bore the Virgin Mary there. In her old age she wanted to go home, and she chose La Palud as a place in which to end her days in prayer and poverty. Before going to Calvary, Jesus, accompanied by Peter and John, went to visit the old lady, and she is reported to have wept tears of blood.

According to the abbé J. Thomas—and his book bears the ecclesiastical imprimatur,—Saint Anne died in Jerusalem; but all historians agree that her remains are not there. According to one legend, when Martha and Mary Magdalene were run out of Judea, they took with them the sacred body, in a boat which traveled without sails, oars, or rudder, and, even more miraculously, landed them the next day at Marseilles. The relic was confided to Saint Auspice, the first bishop of Apt, because this village, separated from the sea by three mountain chains, was regarded as a safe repository. The saint properly hid it during the invasions of the Visigoths and Saracens. "Le malheur est que la cachette était ignorée de tous." The *Bréviaire aptésien* relates that Charlemagne, on his return from Spain—after that fatal battle of his nephew Roland,—assisted at the Easter mass in 792. Suddenly a young man, blind and deaf, entered the church, "guided as if by an invisible hand," and made signs that a certain flagstone should be raised. Of course, the relics were found, and the young man was properly rewarded by restoration to his full faculties. For four hundred years the body was kept in the crypt at Apt, and many popes and kings came to ask for help and favors. In 1392 the remains of the saint were moved to a new chapel in Paris, beside the cathedral. The good abbé proceeds to relate the partitioning of various relics among the churches of France. Thus the humble chapel of Sainte-

Anne-de-la-Palud received a portion, which was finally taken to Rome in 1922. The abbé Thomas, whose account is as nearly complete as any I have found, quotes from Corbière several times in his descriptions of the chapel and the Pardon.

The poem can be divided into four definitely distinct parts, which I indicate arbitrarily by small roman numerals. Thus we have: part i, the description of the figures of the Holy Family in the chapel; part ii, the *Cantique spirituel* itself, almost a hymn in honor of the saint; part iii, a fine vigorous sketch of the visiting pilgrims and a catalogue of the sick and infirm, more in the manner of Goya than of Chaucer; and finally, in part iv, the appearance of the wandering singer of popular tales, from whom the poem has its first name. Its double title indicates that the poet intended to use the legendary background and the Pardon itself as a pedestal for this allegory of human misery; and there was undoubtedly a deal of irony in this juxtaposition and arrangement of the poem so as to give it importance as the climax and finale. The poet has wisely played on two strong emotions, piety and pity, which, aside from this poem, are not always coexistent.

i) Familiar as the pictures of the Holy Family may be, here is a new interpretation—and this is exactly Corbière's power: to make the trite seem strangely new and original. This one is certainly realistic and faintly humorous, a relief from the ordinary romanticized and prettified versions to be seen in most churches. Here the saint is carved of wood which has rotted, but she preserves nevertheless her intrinsic wealth, the power to perform miracles. Mary as a distaff is charming. (As a matter of fact, many Semitic women look like this, because the ambiguous, form-concealing burnous is always curved out and full around the hips and drawn in at the ankles; the appearance is very like that of a distaff wound with yarn.) We have all been profoundly shocked, I am sure, at the scant consideration accorded to Joseph by most of the great painters. He is usually shown as a meek little fellow, superannuated, gazing off-stage, with a bored and uninterested attitude which seems to be saying: "After all, how does this concern me? I'm practically a stranger here, myself." But considerately he is given a full-time job later in the poem. The section closes with an indication of the contrast to be expected between the "seraphic choir and songs of the drunks" in the next part.

ii) The canticle is mainly in a dignified, quasi-liturgical measure. Sometimes the reader is aware that the poet may be grinning sardonically behind a mask of assumed piety. Or might it be the smile of a man who conceals an emotion he is ashamed of? One can never be sure with Tristan. In contrast with stanza 2 of part i, the wood of the saint's statue here has suddenly become sound Breton oak. The "mâle virginité" of stanza 3 offers difficulties. Of course, Corbière enjoys putting the words in paradoxical juxtaposition; but one must suppose that "mâle" here means 'masculine' in the sense that Mary's virginity nevertheless produced one of the world's mightiest ideals.

The many provinces and duties of Saint Anne are piously enumerated, and there is a lot of high poetry and pity in this chant. Truly, after Villon and Baudelaire, Corbière shows, without sentimentality, more real sympathy with the disinherited than any other French poet. He often appears to scoff and jibe because he is suffering a tragic catharsis and refuses to confess it openly. (Who has not cursed and laughed sometimes to keep back a sob?) As for the drunks for whom the saint is asked to show special consideration, Le Braz (*Au pays des pardons,* pp. 273–274), calls the annual pilgrimage "one of those safety valves through which these rough creatures blow off the superfluous steam of their repressed spirits." With appalling frankness he reveals later (p. 278) that "the tents were overflowing with drinkers, even with women"! The principal beverage was "Breton champagne, a kind of gaseous lemonade saturated with alcohol." An authority on the matter has assured me that the mixture must have been similar to what is called a "whisky sour" or a "Tom Collins," and he was very loath to believe that either of these mild potations could have produced the effects alleged by Le Braz. As for tented women at these three-day camp meetings, my Aunt Margaret of Covington once murmured to my father that at similar local gatherings perhaps "more souls were made than were saved."

But that forty-cent candle in the final stanza—so typically *celtique* that the giver remembers the exact price and quotes it, too, right at the saint's ear!

iii) Gourvil (*En Bretagne,* pp. 150–155) has some good photographs of the modern pilgrimages, and his writing is equally graphic. Peasants in costume, beggars, dogs, banners, and floats with images carried by sweating penitents who are winning grace and merit through this labor, peddlers, rhapsodists, cripples, and invalids—all come to this annual Pardon. The widows carry extinguished candles as symbols that the light of their lives has gone out. But a candle may be lighted again. Booths are set up, and the occasion takes on much of the stir and gaiety of a fair. The pilgrims, Gourvil continues, usually bring along tents, made mostly from old sails—beautifully colored, weather-beaten canvas. These Pardons are anticipated throughout the year, and nobody would dream of missing one.

The *vide latus* is apparently a paraphrase (or inexact reminiscence) of John 20: 25 ff., where Jesus directs the doubting Thomas, ". . . behold my hands; and reach hither thy hand and thrust it into my side." From here on, the poet allows his bitterness against sickness and deformity—something very personal is here involved—to force him into one of those violations of good taste of which his critics accused him. He has bitten into his subject as acid eats into the copper plate for an etching; the result is as vivid and horrible as some of the pictures by Félicien Rops, who would have made an excellent illustrator for the whole volume. Yet at times the verses sing along gaily, almost like a popular song; then they are suddenly bleated forth, as if by some recently converted sheep; or they are spat out, like an oath, or gnashed, like mutterings of revenge. But there is none of the coolly planned, more cruel type of deliberate gut-wringing which Laforgue would have fetched in. Corbière sputters because he is angry. He is angry with God for permitting such miseries and agonies to exist. He indicts God, and of course he is knocked off with the next batch of sparrows. As Mephisto said of God, "Economical He is not." (*Faust* II.) France could well have spared a dozen less valid poets, who went on smugly writing until twenty volumes enabled them to get their noses over the sill of the Academy. But Tristan was not allowed to fulfill his destiny.

Saint-Guy is the French equivalent of Saint Vitus, the patron saint of sufferers from the disease. The mistletoe has long been a religious symbol, whether or not because it is parasitical I cannot say. Idiots were commonly said to have been "visited by the Angel Gabriel." The scrofula, which gave its victims those skin blemishes which are here ironically referred to as "fleurs de lis," was formerly called the "king's evil" because it was thought that the touch of a sovereign cured the sufferer. Mlle Laure des Cherres gave me the meaning of the two Breton words: *Ankokrignets* is a combination of *ankou* (*un révenant, fantôme*) and *krignets* (*un infirme, un grognon*), a sickly grumbler. *Kakous* are decrepit old people. The last line of part iii is especially Corbière's. He couldn't resist a poke at the spiritual shepherd of this mangy flock.

iv) Now we come to the real subject of the poem, the alien strolling raconteuse. She is almost blind, a gaunt figure who combines many of the attributes of her name. The setting has been well prepared; we have seen the peaceful shrine and heard eulogies sung about the saint; we have seen the sick and unfortunate come to beg intercession; now we are given an idealized and complete summary of the prototype of Misery. She immediately assumes a like proportion to the stature of the saint and takes over the poem; she is even more powerfully effective than Baudelaire's old women: he presents specimens, but Tristan gives us the archetype.

The *Bon Dieu*'s round which she sings are religious statues. In a cemetery, a *Bon Dieu*, in this sense, may be a calvary, or a tomb figure of a Christ or a saint.

Whatever recension of the story of the Magdalene was current at this time, one must imagine that it afforded lurid and piquant situations and ended in a fine scene of regeneration, the foot-bathing, and perhaps her later help in carrying the saint's body to Brittany. She has been painted a hundred times; usually she is lying in a cave, in a dim religious light, reading a presumably edifying book, her eyes red with remorse and turned heavenward for reassurance.

As for the Wandering Jew, Emile Souvestre (*Le Foyer breton,* pp. 107–111) quotes a section from "le vieux *Dialogue du Juif et du bonhomme Misère*" which may have given Corbière an idea: "Listen to me, companions of high or low estate; listen to the words of the two oldest men on earth, two men who are doomed to live until the last judgment. One is called Isaac the traveler; the other, Misery. . . . Near Orleans they met each other, and, as old men will, they spoke. Misery said to Isaac: 'Good morning, Wandering Jew. Where do you come from? What are you doing in the world? You are weary and sad—I can see that.' 'I am walking day and night. God wills it because I displeased him. I am walking night and day and I suffer the greatest of troubles: I cannot die. I must live on until the day of judgment, alas! I thought I was the oldest person on earth, but I see that you are my elder in the sufferings of life.' 'My poor child, you were born yesterday. How many hundred years have you been here? But I count the years by thousands. When our first father Adam disobeyed God, I was born in his house, and since then his children have always fed me, in spite of themselves, at their fireside.' 'Father, what is your name and what is your calling?' 'I'm the old codger Misery. Wherever I pass, I hear weeping. I am the cause of all unhappiness and the father of all crime. You ought to know me, for the human race has cried my name ever since I was born. I have made man suffer all evils and have tried on him every torture.' 'Oh, if it's you who torture people, I know you. For seventeen hundred years I've been hearing about you. You are the spirit of evil on the earth. But at least, you crazy old man, why don't you enter the houses of the rich? Why prefer the roofs of the poor, under which they never eat anything but bread?' 'Be quiet, Jew! I hope soon to make a tour among the rich. If I can once get in a house, I'm not easily chased out.' 'Your clothes are much too worn, you wicked old man; you can't be received in their homes. If they saw you before the door, you'd be chased away. You can do it among the poor.' 'I know how to make poor folk out of the rich, O Jew! I enter the house of the mightiest by fraud. There are already two servants there whom I know and they'll open the door for me: Prodigality and Idleness.' 'Farewell, demon. Your looks curdle my blood. Begone, wicked old man, we have nothing to settle together. I have a torturer stronger than you, for I am under the very hand of God!' "

The story of Abelard's meteoric career and downfall has been embalmed in the pure amber of literature by the coöperator himself in his *Historia calamitatum,* and much of it even more beautifully in the wonderful letters of Héloïse, "that learned nun," which are the greatest document of womanly passion and devotion ever written—and I am not unaware of the works of Sappho, Corinna, Anyte, Vittoria Colonna, Gaspara Stampa, Saint Theresa, Hroswitha, Louise Labé, Sor Juana Inés de la Cruz, and Emily Dickinson at her own very brief best.

This poem is the masterpiece of the book, and its emotional gamut is unbelievably broad. Love and piety are contrasted sharply with a pity whetted by indignation and irony. Even in the midst of the more realistic horrors that are enumerated, there gleam some flashes of the comedy of life, sometimes tender, occasionally bawdy. Saint Anne is always admirable and noble in the way that the humblest peasant might be superior to some diseased and tyrannic seigneur; as honest copper is superior to thin-washed gold. Joseph is always the butt of a sly but harmless humor. The fifty-nine quatrains are in the simple ballad measure, but the effect is never monotonous. Often each stanza compacts an incident and has a climax in its last line. In fact, the poet saves his punches for a series of carefully planned exits. You will be surprised to find how many shocks or smiles you will get from those fourth lines on a rereading.

The skillful contrast of the "seraphic choir and songs of the drunks" at the end of part i indicates the method employed throughout. The marks of suffering on the saint's face, made by tears of blood and tears of love, and the pathos of a woman's old age—the drained, exhausted breasts—suddenly are forgotten in the lofty dignity with which she confronts the Almighty himself, or the natural humanity with which she bediapers a moist brat, or aids a cow in calfbirth. I certainly feel better acquainted with the old lady than with any other saint in the calendar. A "woman of a stirring life" she must be, for she finds time to comfort and protect an unmarried mother, start the drunks safely homeward, hustle the dead soldiers and sailors along toward heaven, and keep an eye on "Joseph-concierge." Yet the only reward she receives is the humble distaff of flax and that very expensive candle with which the poet bows himself out, after slipping in a word, gratis, recommending himself to the Holy Trinity.

This hymn establishes a lofty note in the dignity of plainsong or of a well-sung mass. And part iii creeps in so patly that, before the reader notices it, he finds himself wincing at the catalogue of horrors and disgusting afflictions. Yet, by virtue of the subject, these creatures rightly belong here. This is the Day of the Pardon, the annual convention of sinners and sufferers. Corbière has dragged in nothing *per se* just to be nasty. One feels that sometimes Baudelaire went out hunting for something unpleasant to record, but Tristan had presumably grown up with these yearly Pardons, and only when their full impact had matured in his ironic soul did he write his indictment against God—for that is what the piece actually is. Certainly Verlaine never achieved anything of comparable magnitude; Mallarmé's "Hérodias" and "Après-midi d'un faune" are artificial stuff in comparison; Valéry's "La Jeune Parque" is, as he called it, an "exercise"; Rimbaud's "Bateau ivre" is a precocious and prodigious, purely imaginary, *tour de force,* and only "Les Petites Vieilles" and "Le Voyage" of Baudelaire can offer the "Pardon" any serious competition in French poetry since 1857! It is a vitriolic bomb flung smack in the face of God; yet even the Inquisition could hardly have proved the poet guilty of blasphemy, for the effects are achieved by innuendo rather than by direct statement.

If, on this so broad pedestal, a block of stone with carvings of angels, saints, beggars, kings, and ornamented with the blood and pus of all imaginable diseases and deformities, enriched by the homely picture of the life of a Breton woman with a child on her knees, spinning beside the evening hearth; if, on this solid four-sided monolith, the thin figure of the final heroine, Misery, seems small, backed up though she be by the calvary silhouetted on the skyline, this is by no means a technical mistake. In his alembic the poet has refined all the misfortunes and sorrows, all the diseases and sufferings, and he has presented them in an allegorical being that both mocks at and wrings the heart. This walking Misery, shag-toothed, with her old knapsack and her empty pipe, seems to me a more terrible personage than any who have come to the Pardon. (This is on the principle that a heartache can hurt worse than a toothache.) And that final stanza, with the scooped-out smile on the furrowed face, as the creature makes the sign of the cross (with a mangy hand), is a fine climax.

I have seen the Pardon twice and it did not let me down completely, though but few beggars, invalids, and cripples were to be seen. I found only one strolling singer, a blind man whose songs seemed rather mediocre. I had lunch with him in a tent *bistro* and he paid me the compliment of asking me to help him identify the paper money and count his take. It amounted to about five dollars for three hours' work, and he was pleased. Certainly he was nothing comparable to Corbière's Misery. On the night of the procession of candles, everyone had a taper, protected from the wind by a paper cup. We marched in a circle about a half mile in circumference and sang hymns and masses to the accompaniment of the program broadcast from the belfry. Some twenty thousand slept in the open air on the ground that night, in a nice comfortable cow pasture. All the Breton pilgrims very realistically fetched along roast chicken and boiled hams, and there was no end of drinking booths where cider, wine, and beer could be had. Improvidentially, I lived two days on pears, grapes, and tomatoes, for the two small hotels in town were swamped with women and babies. The next day, mass was conducted continuously for hours. Every once in a while the music would stop and a matter-of-fact voice would announce over a loud-speaker: A child in a red jacket has been found under the altar; parents please identify. A pocketbook has been found by the west portal. An old lady has fainted in the chancel. Et cetera. Then the mass would proceed in full swing. Seven bishops in full regalia were in the procession, and the many villages were represented by groups in costume with stiffly laundered headdresses, a different style for each community. One person died, another was born; but since there were, according to the press, a hundred thousand people present, that is not a high average. Undoubtedly, many tender unions were made and sealed that night under the balmy skies and pandering stars. I could find none of the church décor mentioned by the poet. The Saint Anne I saw was a very much bedizened image who was teaching the young Virgin to read. St. Joseph was nowhere in evidence. Nor could I find any of the "Breton champagne" mentioned by Le Braz.

The emotional impact of the reality was far less than I had felt on first reading the poem. But that is exactly the function of art: it hits harder.

Cris d'aveugle, p. 138—

Immediately following the vision of Misery, like one of her most stalwart retainers, this blindman gives the final turn to the thumbscrew of this section. Our nerves have been worn out and we have no more resistance. The poem is designed, by lack of punctuation, to give the effect of a continuous wailing cry. (Incidentally, I believe this was the first poem in modern French literature to be printed that way. It sired, alas! the final work of the susceptible Mallarmé and the poems of his willing disciple, Stefan George; and as a result of their influence there is many a poet in France, England, and America today who by omitting to punctuate obfuscates further his obscurities.)

"Ann hini goz," the name of the air to which the words are to be sung, means "the old woman."

Good church Latin is used in stanza 2, and in stanza 3 we have the cry of Christ on the cross: "My God, My God, why hast thou forsaken me?" For line 5 of stanza 3, Ida Levi (p. 242) has discovered in one of Corbière's personal copies of the first edition an interesting variant: instead of "Colombes de la Mort," the revised line reads "Noirs poulets de la Mort"—a change I have not cared to reproduce.

It is needless to comment on the piling up of miseries the poet has here achieved. The really horrible picture of the eaten-out eyes is the climax; for those "burning tears of sulphur" are nothing, frankly, but vicious pus. Once I was led by a young guide, whom I had met in the gloomy interior of the mosque of Sidi 'Okba at Kairouan, the sacred city of Tunisia, up the winding stairs of the tower. When we came out in the open, he said: "Voilà, m'sieu, la perspective!" I gazed over miles of desert beyond the flat rooftops of the city—I seemed to be looking clear to infinity! But it was only then I noticed that my guide had only two hollow sockets, with flabby eyelids which flickered over them. It certainly ruined "la perspective" for me.

The poem is built on six-line stanzas, and the fifth and sixth lines repeat substantially the first and second; they all rhyme on a strong masculine French rhyme: "mort, encor, *misericors,* corps, sabord, bord, d'or, mord, tord, sort, dort, dehors, remords, encor, d'Armor, fort, sort, nord, cor." This gives a monotonous effect which I cannot hope to reproduce in English. It is the endless repetition of a sound not dissimilar to that which Poe maintained was the most melancholy of all vocal noises (see "The Raven" and the essay on its composition). Line 24: "Rouge comme un sabord" comes from Edouard Corbière's novel *Le Négrier,* p. 34: " . . . ce joli navire . . . ses sabords peints de rouge . . . "

The tight emotional effect of the book as a whole has culminated; now we shall put to sea, toward the finale. Though the sea poems are great in spots, the ocean is less than a man, and it is of men that ARMOR was written.

⋄   ⋄   ⋄

I cannot leave this section without including a few illustrations of the Bretons' attitude toward death. This is not as gratuitous as it might seem,

224

for both sections are morbid here and there, and death is a haunting thing in Brittany.

Simon Davaugour, in his *Sous le ciel gris,* has a macabre yarn in the style of Poe which shows much the same gruesome spirit as does Corbière's catalogue of the sick and crippled, as well as the Celtic spirit of making the best of a situation. A traveler is caught in a shower of rain and takes refuge in the house of an old Breton. "You're soaked to the hide. Come dry yourself at this fire of boards," says his host, and goes out of the room. The guest dries his clothes before a "great fire, an immense, triumphal fire, really absurd for so miserable a hovel." But it is a strange fire, full of hallucinations, and finally the visitor begins to believe he is looking at a pile of marvelous and terrifying things: skulls without teeth, sockets without eyeballs, twisted arms, and shriveled flesh. The old man returns with a fresh armload of rotten boards and explains to the pallid guest: "I forgot to tell you . . . I am the sexton. I would have nothing at all to burn if my business didn't supply me wood gratis. These boards are from coffins which I dig up when the time has come." (Perhaps I should mention here that a French slang phrase for a burial ground is "the turnip patch.")

There is something almost awesome about the cemetery round a church in a small Breton village, for the number of graves often exceeds the number of living inhabitants: it is a kind of eternal citadel amid a transitory town, and everyone has presumably dozens of dead ancestors there. He can drop in any time and enjoy a melancholy hour of meditation and prayer. I have often seen widows praying with one eye closed and meanwhile keeping track of passers-by so as not to miss anything.

The mottoes and inscriptions in the God's acres of Brittany are very edifying. As usual, one finds *Memento mori, Respice finem,* "All good people who pass by, / pray God for those who herein lie!" And couplets in Breton: "Hirio dime, / Varhoaz dide" (My turn today, tomorrow yours). Others, in peculiar French, say: "O sinners, repent while you live, because for us who are dead there is no time for that"; and "It is folly and improvidence to hope—you will die when your time comes." How much all this resembles Dante's terrible "Lasciate ogni speranza" (Abandon *all* hope). In the ossuary at Roche-Maurice there is a statue of a skeleton bearing an arrow; the inscription reads: "Je vous tue tous" (I slay you all). In many towns the ossuary is joined to the church or is in its immediate vicinity. The one in Roscoff, built in the style of Louis XIII, with large square columns and arches, has no door, and entrance is made by way of the windows. I tried it.

225

There is a Breton song which used to be chanted when the parish made a solemn procession to the ossuaries at Toussaint (All Souls' Eve—November 1):

Decomp dar garnel, Kristenien, guelomp ar relegou
Euz hon breuder, c'hoarezet, hon tadou, hon mammou . . .

which means: "Come to the charnel house, Christians. Contemplate the relics—of our brothers and sisters, our fathers and mothers . . . " And it continues: "Here are neither riches, nobility, nor beauty.—Alas, to this lamentable state you see the dead are come—their very silence speaks more loudly than the eloquence of the living."

But bones are no longer kept in the ossuaries; some recent health regulation forbids. In few cemeteries are any noteworthy number of graves protected by the right of "perpetual concession." Thus every few years it is necessary to exhume the occupants who have been there longest, in order to make room for the newcomers. When this is done, the slab itself is returned to the surviving family, by which, as time goes past, it is almost certain to be put to some practical use: a bench outside a door, a stepping stone before the entrance, or even a handy table top in the kitchen. I was told that one baker had used the slab of his great-grandfather for a mixing board. And what harm in that?

Anatole Le Braz (*La Légende de la mort chez les bretons armoricains,* Vol. I, pp. 357–363) has a true story with which this gloomy section may be concluded. The curé of Penvénan asked the sexton, one Poaz-Coz, to exhume a certain body in order to make room for a new customer. The sexton replied that the dead man had been big and fat and would not be "ready" yet. But the poor man had to obey his superior. Well, it happened that while he was digging, his pick . . . and that night the sexton received a visitation from the dead man's spirit. "You see what they have done to me!" Finally a compromise was effected: the unwilling ravisher of the tomb promised to have some masses said, and the spirit forgave him. But the curé had an appropriate stroke of apoplexy and died *tout de suite.—Voilà!*

GENS DE MER

I am sorry to have been able to do so little with these poems; but the reckless jargon, the idioms, the vocabulary of maritime terms, and the willful snytax are very difficult. Just when I thought I was sailing along most bouncingly, I have been stalled by a calm, have run aground on a hidden linguistic shoal, or have been hoisted off in a wink by a bravura of rhetoric like a squall! For many words I have found no help in the dictionaries. The use of argot, dialect, and even of the five-letter words (*we* call them the four-letter words) has often obfuscated me.

Every coastal Breton is a sailor, a sailor's wife, or has maritime aspirations. Pierre Loti's *Pêcheur d'Islande* gives a fine description of the hard and dangerous lives of the people; but Tristan, also a sailor, has chosen to present a more reckless and humorous aspect—even when he is dealing with the stark tragedy of the sea. He does not hesitate to mock in the very face of death by shipwreck, or to use a lighthouse as a phallic symbol. Synge, in *Riders to the Sea* and *The Aran Islands,* makes one aware of the affinity between these two Celtic peoples, the Irish and the Bretons—it was perhaps this that drew me subconsciously toward Tristan; but while Synge works in tragedy or plain realism, Corbière, though equally factual, usually grins.

Maybe I can save enough of the sharp tang of the brine and the iodine smell on the wind to make a reader itch to get at the originals for himself. Our poet must have learned the nautical idiom at his father's knees, or from some old sailor turned fisherman, who liked to pass on his lingo to a willing young stripling. Remember, too, that the boy had his own boat at a tender age and sailed when and where he pleased. His physical handicaps prevented his being much of a hero ashore, but once he was in his element he stopped at nothing. With sheet and tiller in his hands, he could cherish such illusions of pelagic conquest that Odysseus would have loved him as a brother. A lone sailor in a small boat in even a mild storm becomes, to himself at least, a minor demigod, although sometimes a scared and meek one. Nor is this mere conjecture on my part. The solemn Le Goffic and Martineau record it as hearsay that Tristan was a fearless, even a foolhardy, sailor.

Aside from the phonies in "Aurora," which I do not translate, Tristan's sailors are authentically portrayed. They are by no means to be confused with those uniformed blatant little landlubbers who cluttered our coast towns during the last war: untrained shavelings who didn't know an elephant clip, vang, gimbal, pelorus, flam, paravane, skeg, fidley, diaper plate, bon jean curve, paulin, padeye, pawl, or scrieve board from a day shape! They didn't even know azimuth from syzygy! But these Breton sailors have been tanned by a thousand winds and are salted like herrings. They chew an eternal quid; they are tough, fearless in danger, and they use dirty words—they would be nothing for a Wave to go out with. Several critics have correctly noted that Corbière's "La Fin," intentionally a rectification of Hugo's "Oceano nox," restores the life and death of sailors to reality.

227

After "La Rapsode foraine," this is the second masterwork of the book. It has all the material for tragedy: the little hero, the tragic flaw of lust which destroys him, the emotions of pity awakened in a reader—at least, of the original,—and the ironic finale, death for "this body which has known ... love." But Corbière, as ever, has added his macabre and sinister touches, until the result is almost pure horror. He has deliberately heaped up—as if from a thesaurus—more than a dozen synonyms and variants for "twisted": the two title words *bossu* and *bitor,* and, thereafter, *tors* and *retors, cordée, bosse en la tête, tordu, hâler, bosco* (a slang word for "hunch-back"), *biscornue, tire-bouchon, tortillard, crochard, tortillou.* The whole poem writhes and twists, like an Aubrey Beardsley drawing. It suggests that Corbière is externalizing his own arthritic gnarlings. Rousselot says the sea poems were written between 1861 and 1868, and that they are of a "réalisme brutal." He warns that this one is "not a poem for young girls"; but then, M. Rousselot is a Frenchman, and French girls are not yet emancipated as are our *Backfische.*

Notice the many nautical terms used, aside from those naturally implicit in the subject: the girls are to be had "by tonnage"; their nicknames are only such as sailors could bestow; they are "rigged" in suitable clothes; the girl called Mary-Saloppe (a *marie-salope,* slut, prostitute, is also a dredger's mud-barge) complains that it is "not her watch"; Bitor is "careened"; his cries are like the shriek of a ship's pulleys. Some of the language is rough. The reader must have tolerance—especially if he is familiar with several writers who do not use blanks to fill out certain words. Line 49: "Loustic" is an interesting loan from the German "lustig," meaning "very happy and full of animal spirits." "Gouine," farther on, is taken from the name of Nell Gwynn, Charles II's mistress—so French argot scholars say; the latest argot dictionary gives it a specific meaning, but the older ones include it with general terms for easy women. Corbière takes his words where he finds them.

"Gardiens de pur contour," in the description of Bitor's breeches, is twisted from the "gardiens du contour pur" of Gautier's poem, "L'Art," in *Emaux et Camées.*

"Ciel moutonné ... " is an old popular saying (cf. *Comédie des proverbes,* 1636): "A mackerel sky means a quick change to worse weather, as make-up betrays that a beauty is fast losing her bloom."

The catalogue of heroes who symbolize Bitor's mood on the fatal evening includes a variety of gallants. Of Lauzun, courtier and general, La Bruyère

said that "his life was like a romance, except that it lacked probability."
Lagardère, a hunchbacked cloak-and-sword hero, was the creation of the
prolific romancer Paul Féval *père,* and appeared both in a novel, *Le Bossu*
(1857), and in a romantic melodrama of the same name (1862). Alain Char-
tier, a poet renowned in his day, was confidential secretary to two French
kings, Charles VI and VII. The anecdote that brings him into Corbière's
poem is this: Margaret of Scotland, the first wife of the Dauphin (later
Louis XI), one day seeing Chartier asleep in a chair, ran up and kissed him.
Now he was anything but handsome, though a witty fellow, and when the
princess was asked why she had bestowed on him so unexpected a favor,
she answered that she had kissed not the man, but the mouth which had
uttered so many golden words—a tribute any poet would be glad of. Bitor
is supposed to be proceeding very gaily toward the tryst, but in his de-
formity he suggests the court jester of Louis XII, Triboulet, also a cripple.
The Mayeux of some twenty lines further on is a type of French caricature,
created by Charles Traviès; he is deformed, sensual, and witty, a mixture
of Panurge and Polichinelle.

As one of earth's disinherited, Bitor immediately enlists Corbière's sym-
pathy, and this is strengthened by the mutual physical malformation of
the poet and the hero. Whether or not Bitor had once been normal and
owned a plantation and boat is beside the question. After forty years as a
ship's boy, he is resigned to his simple pleasures of being topman when
everyone else is ashore, and to his annual binge. Corbière's real irony is
shown when he has Bitor stretch "tout de son long," at full length, on a
coil of rope, and when he sticks his head in the door, at the height of a dog
lugged out of church by the scuff of the neck. The madam asks "How
many are you?" because his back seems to follow close after him like an-
other person.

Corbière does not hesitate to use religious terms for any purpose that
suits him, as when the red light of the brothel is called *Stella maris,* the
Virgin's title as patron of sailors. When Bitor is called "Limonadier de la
Passion," the reference may be to him who reached up vinegar on a sponge
to Jesus on the cross. (Matt. 27: 48; *et al.*)

How accurately the poet has hit off the various nationalities in a couplet!
Especially the Yankees, the Chinese, and the Germans. In that congress of
nations in the lupanar, I am happy to note that no Scots are included. Such
a "corkscrew" hero as Bitor deserves the top wench of the establishment,
the most popular of the evening with ten customers on her towel hook. The
explanation of the roughhouse is apparently that the girls are annoyed that

a hunchback should have his pleasure with one of them. The blanket tossing was an established custom in the times of Don Quixote and Goya. This is not a fatal punishment, so it must be assumed that Bitor's shame at being exposed naked to the jibes of the girls and probably the feeling that his life had hit an emotional climax led him, in the course of the emotional reaction following, to throw himself into the sea. The impact of this poem is, it seems to me, stronger than that achieved in any of Baudelaire's terrible visions.

Bambine, p. 172—

It was the first line that smote me: "You sleep beneath the parsnips . . . " Who wouldn't want to read more? Only Corbière could have approached a poem like that. Very well, the sightseers on a pleasure trip meet a storm. A pretty woman is bored and wants to get off. (She has stepped right out of Vol. VII, chap. ii, of *Tristram Shandy:* "Captain, quoth she, for heaven's sake, let us get ashore.") Other passengers have addressed Bambine correctly as "commandant"—the officer in command of a French ship, whatever his exact title may be, is always thus addressed: it is the equivalent of "Sir,"— but this person calls him "conducteur," as if he were a guard on an excursion train, or a bus conductor. Naturally he is annoyed. "Well, well! So you'd like to go ashore?" What he is thinking is: Who the hell wouldn't, in this storm? There is no reason to apologize for his frank statement to the woman, or for a couple of words which we all know in English but seldom say to strangers.

Au vieux Roscoff, p. 176—

In 1870 this was a town of two thousand inhabitants, mostly fishermen, kelp-burners, and—all of them—sailors. The storm-beaten promontory juts into the Channel halfway between Brest and Saint-Malo. In former days its harbor offered ideal headquarters for the buccaneers and smugglers, because Plymouth, Portland, and Portsmouth lie just forty miles to the north. The isolationist's hatred of England and Spain crops out in this poem. In stanza 2 I had to fudge by substituting "Cyclops" for "borgne," in reference to the one-eyed lighthouse. Stanza 3: in the Marine Biology Laboratory in Roscoff I finally got an interpretation of "margats": "margat" is the popular name for the great northern diver, the ember-goose, *Colymbis immer,* or *glacialis.* In stanza 4, "en friture" is the image seen by a sharp eye and swift whimsy: a frying of the surf, like hot deep fat! In stanza 7 one of those lovable difficulties of French pops up: "ans" and "années," like "larme" and "pleur," offer an embarrassing richness, but in English we have no such handy synonyms. The flowering sea-rushes in the rust-gnawed cannon have occasioned difficulties. They must have belonged to the Potamogetonaceae— perhaps they were *Ruppia maritima* or *Zostera nana*. They might even have been *Juncus acutus* or *Juncus Gerardi!* Naturally, I wanted to see for myself, and spent hours poking around in every possible cove and climbing little promontories where the cannon should have been. Finally an old sailor took me out on one of the new jetties and there it was: buried in cement, with plugged muzzle, sans flowers, and in use as a bollard!

Of Roscoff in the poet's day, Arnoux (*Une âme et pas de violon,* chap. iv) writes romantically, as is his fashion; but he has a few fine phrases and images which sound authentic enough: "Here with its spitting shoals and rocky reefs is a strange kitchen garden entrusted to the sea. At the same time a land of tempests and mild climate, assaulted by furious waves, but always preserving an equable temperature, a coast for shipwrecks and for early vegetables, a mosaic of fields enclosed by low walls, a peninsula of cloisonné, without trees; the cauliflower flourishes, the artichoke thrusts forth its leaves from hell, trenchant as steel, its beds of torture; onions make their tubular gardens, potatoes . . . " et cetera. "It is a rare country, whence the farmer does not hesitate to take his crop across the salt treacherous water" (to sell in England). Arnoux also describes (apparently he could in his time discover more authentic remnants than are apparent today) the veteran pirates, finally pensioned by the government for sound work against the English navy; and he is no doubt right in insisting that the young sailor had actual contact with old buccaneers, smugglers, and slave traders. Certainly the boy's father, by that time a wealthy and respected citizen, did much to keep alive the memory of the good old days he had known at first hand.

According to both writers, old Roscoff and the life of a sailor of those times were much richer in color and incident. The old captain complained that "le romantisme et la vapeur ont tué l'art des vers et la navigation à voile, la seule véritable": two most sound conclusions. Arnoux continues with a discussion of the effect of the father's advice to his son about the reading of poetry aloud, mentions the old gentleman's sound disapproval of the poetry of Hugo because it was merely rhetoric, and concludes the chapter with the suggestion that Tristan really learned his art directly from his contact with the sea, "genèse éternelle des formes."

Roscoff today has given up most of its former fishing trade, but the vegetables still thrive, and the principal crop seems to be English summer

231

tourists, for the town is just across the Channel. In truth, the atmosphere during two Augusts I have been there did breathe excessively of

> women with teeth, and dismal legs, in plaids,
> puny dogs with jackets, in their laps;
> knock-kneed girls in shorts, bright Nelson-lads,
> High Anglicans in tweeds and spats and caps.

The tides seem to have become increasingly lower, and I have seen little use of the new breakwater lately installed. One has usually to walk half a mile from the original coast to do any crab or clam hunting, or to take a boat to the Ile de Batz, a passage that can still be very dangerous in rough weather. The ossuary has been emptied of the fine specimens of bones, the Corbière house has been turned into a marine biology laboratory, half a dozen modern lighthouses and beacons take the place of the mighty *phare* of other days, the bars are more frequented by rather sleek young town lads than by old salts, Le Gad's inn is now a mercer's store, the hotel once called the Pigeon Blanc is now the Hôtel de France and the doors are locked at eleven, several obviously once fine bistros for sailors now serve tea to elderly ladies, and even the oldest bartenders no longer knew what a "boujaron" really is. Quantum mutatus ab illo!

La Fin, p. 180—

A dozen lines from Hugo's "Oceano nox" preface the poem, from which Corbière does not scruple to borrow several phrases. "Oh, how many seamen, how many captains who went joyously on distant cruises have vanished in that gloomy horizon! ... How many masters are dead with their crews! Ocean has torn all the pages from their lives, and with one breath has scattered them over the water. Nothing is known of their end, lost in the abysm. ... Nothing will know their names, not even the humble stone in the narrow graveyard where the echo answers us, not even a green willow dropping its leaves in autumn, nor even the plaintive and monotonous cries of a blindman who sings by the corner of an old bridge."

But Corbière's heroes have the fine devil-may-care spirit we like to associate with the tars of other days; and the poem has the usual irony, bawdry, and macabre quality that we expect. No one drowns in Baudelaire's "Le Voyage," and Valéry's "Le Cimetière marin" deals only with the serene ocean as a background for the poet's philosophic meditations on death. In the cemeteries of any maritime town are to be found innumerable cenotaphs erected for sailors lost at sea. There are a few drifting corpses in Rimbaud's "Bateau ivre," used purely as ornament. Verlaine wrote of the present poem that it may not contain *all* about the sea, but that it certainly includes all the proud and nostalgic spirit of the sailors; Corbière was, he continues, "the first French poet to make them speak and think in a natural manner." Le Goffic (in his preface to *Les Amours jaunes,* 1926, p. xxvii) raises the question of where the rhetoric begins and ends in the poem. "He has truly a tenderness for the sea, almost like that of a jealous lover; he watches over her as if she were his own property. An explicable passion, for was it not the sea which gave him the only satisfaction for his *amour-propre?* This poor scrap of humanity, who dragged on the land with the clumsiness of a wading bird, with clipped wings, the sea made him the equal of the most robust sailor, a 'fine sprig of a fellow!' "

Line 6: *boujaron,* a ration of brandy (Corbière's note). Line 7: "la *Camarde*" comes from *camus,* a snubnosed person. In the familiar form it means a feminine personification, a noseless skeleton, "grim death."

◇   ◇   ◇

It may seem odd to tack on the following here, after the book is apparently almost finished, but Le Goffic (p. xxviii) joins on so neatly that I must quote from him. Moreover, it will reëstablish the true chronological order in the book, and we must remember that the first half really came after these poems of Brittany and the sea were written. "But it was not the sea which took Corbière. A woman passed, a *parisienne.* Beautiful, young, elegant, and titled [Le Goffic is misinformed about this], she divined the secret so well hidden in his eyes; she loved the poet; but it was too late, and this romantic conjunction of a heroine from Feuillet [a sentimental, romantic novelist, 1821–1890] and a Triton from the seas of Brittany did not enrich with a brilliant chapter the sentimental literature of the nineteenth century. The fault was on neither side, perhaps, it was life's: happiness demands an apprenticeship which Corbière had not served." Tristan's semi-literary cousin, Pol Kalig, said that the poet was "a tender repressed personality." His unfortunate physique and illness had developed "instincts of anarchy which awakened in his inner depths all the Celtic strain." (Le Goffic, p. xxix.)

I must say that if the poet had to be wrecked, I would have preferred it to have been the sea, for this stimulated the more unique side of his work. No man who has sailed a boat can afford to miss these poems of the seas and sailors of Brittany. I have just reread in Heredia's *Trophées* the section "La Mer de Bretagne." Those poems are beautiful, in a calm static fashion,

233

like fine paintings; but they have nothing of the sharp salt and the lash of the wind; there is no excitement of danger and no real getting into the thing itself, as are to be found in "La Goutte" (not translated here) and "La Fin."

RONDELS POUR APRES

This slight group of poems foreshadows what a second volume, the proposed "Mirlitons," might have been. Le Goffic (in his preface to the edition of 1926, pp. xxx–xxxi) is worth quoting: "What would this book have been? A replica of the first part of *Amours jaunes?* I fear so, after the two pieces which have already appeared." (Apparently Le Goffic did not revise his preface of 1912—because the edition of 1926, now before me, prints *five* examples.) "For us [he continues] the true Corbière is not there, in spite of the strange music which resounds briefly, so sweet and harrowing that it makes one dream of that bird of which Renan speaks: the bird that saws the heart with a diamond saw. The Corbière we cherish is above all the poet of 'Armor' and 'Gens de mer,' the uneven poet, powerful and delicious, sincere even to brutality and suddenly showing an unexpected tenderness, as in the example of the disused cannon in his 'Vieux Roscoff,' which gave room for an ingenuous tuft of flowering sea-rushes in its iron throat." The other critics come through with nothing, except Arnoux, who writes (in his preface to the edition of 1947): "Do we dare conclude a study, even a hasty one which proceeds too much by allusions and evocations, which lacks, to my great shame, the proper basis and critical apparatus, without mentioning 'Rondels pour après'? Five pieces in all, short, with the most aerial resonance. Tristan humanizes, softens himself, puts a mute in his instrument. And this brutal breaker of strings draws from it the most imponderable melodies. Verlaine himself never equaled this ease with which Corbière moves in a world of nuances, of echoes, which no longer depends on gravity. Death approaches; a light and melancholy mist deafens the violences, draws out and unites the piercing tones into a subtle harmony, a froth (*frottis*) of dreams...." He has not done very well by the rondels, this M. Arnoux.

No, the critics have accorded scant justice to these fugitive pieces. They are the final lyric gasps of a dying man. They are almost coughed forth, and there are bloodflecks on them! What makes them all the more pathetic is that the poet is still mocking, though the froth of death is on his lips. There is a supermundane airy sweetness about them that has been equaled in lyrical poetry only by some of the songs of Shakespeare and the early poems of Blake. Even the almost meaningless evocations which begin several of them: "enfant, voleur d'étincelles" (child, thief of sparks), "méchant ferreur de cigales" (naughty blacksmith of the cicadas), and "léger peigneur de comètes" (nimble comber of comets)—even these fumblings in the abacadabra of poetry, these almost charlatan attempts to get a *spirituel* rabbit from a matter-of-fact prose hat, are powerful assertions of the legerdemain of the man. Yet there is a gravity about them, for they are hallowed by the radiant majesty of death.

Sonnet posthume, p. 186—

Violating, as it does, the title of the section, why was this included? Only a profoundly ironic spirit could have written it: a man doomed and aware of it, who shrugs and grins and says, "So what?" It is a sequel to "Epitaphe." He is talking to his body, somewhat in the manner of the many medieval dialogues between Soul and Body, especially that by Villon. "L'Autre" of line 3 is the forever unattainable woman of our dreams, more effective because she is not real. Verlaine in *Fêtes galantes,* 1869, had already written, "Je ... vous décroche une étoile," in "Sur l'herbe"; probably this stimulated "décrocheur d'étoiles." But it's not so very criminal to steal from one's brother. Lines 7 and 8 are similarly indebted to Baudelaire's spiders in "Spleen" (iv), and his "Danse macabre" has the ancestor of that angel on the ceiling. The final tercet reminds one of the gravediggers in *Hamlet,* and the snuffing of the light by the sacristan sounds vaguely like the fate of Desdemona. The gratuitous biff to the nose of the corpse completes the catalogue of sadistic tricks heaped up in the book. But the French grew up, in the Middle Ages, with the Dance of Death painted on their houses, and with the open charnelhouse of the Innocents by the Tour Saint-Jacques, in the middle of Paris. They even used to take Sunday walks there to enjoy the sights. Villon mentions several times that he and his companions used to take a cold bird, a cool bottle, and a hot wench out to Montfaucon for a pleasant picnic supper—and this was the city scaffold! The French have stout stomachs.

Rondel, p. 188—

Childish, almost without meaning, this little poem has a magic, indefinable, light as thistledown, evanescent as a bubble. The bears that throw a pavingstone are borrowed from the one in La Fontaine (the tenth fable in book VIII) which crushed a fly on the friendly old amateur gardener's

nose by smashing it—and the man too—with a "pavé." This may compli-
cate matters even more. The meaning doesn't matter—it is the music—
Verlaine's "la musique devant toute chose." *That* matters! memorize it,
sing it, love it—and you will have here some of the secret of Corbière's
charm. All these rondels are self-valedictory wavings of the hand: he is
giving himself a going-away party. His hand is at his lips, bidding adieu.

None of these alleged "rondels" is true to the form originated by the
troubadours. Corbière has capriciously knocked off a line or so, and cut
some of the wearisome refrains—to my mind, an improvement on the form.
I wonder what the delicate, porcelain genius of Austin Dobson would have
made of these rondels. I wish he had had a crack at translating them, but
it is doubtful if any Victorian could have made heads or tails of Tristan.
Like a medlar, or a Chinese egg, such poets as he want time for ripening
before consumption.

Do, l'enfant, do…, p. 190—

This one follows logically enough. The Italian salutations move progres-
sively from early evening to the final good-night. My line 5 will remind
anyone of "Fear no more the heat o' the sun…" *Fesse-cahier* is a term
of denigration applied to any mere drudge of the pen, a bank clerk, lawyer's
copyist, or, as Corbière means here, a hack reviewer. Cf. Goethe's "Prok-
tophantasmist" in "Walpurgis Nacht," *Faust* I. The French call gossamer
"the thread of the Virgin," which is doubly charming when one considers
that our English word came from "goose summer," the season when geese
were eaten and cobwebs drifted about. An essential difference between
the two peoples is here revealed: for one, the belly; to the other, the spirit.
Tristan never lets his reader forget the universal hatred of the philistine
for the artist. Even most of our modern college administrators do not
understand the importance of the creative artist—in any field whatever—
as he might be related to education.

Mirliton, p. 192—

Just how Tristan hit on the cicadas would be hard to say. The locust is
the symbol of Provence, to be found on buildings, jewelry, embroideries,
etc. During its musical period the insect does not eat at all, simply because
its mouth is indicated merely by a sealed cross that does not open. The
eternal shrill tintinnabulation to be heard in summer over the whole
province is caused by vibrating membranes on the underside of the abdo-
men. The blacksmith mentioned by the poet might imply someone who

helped file the scraper or beat out the plates with which the almost metallic noise is made. One must avoid the notion that the winged creature needs shoeing, like a horse. The *muguet* is the flower that all France uses for May Day, when every market place is literally white with the bouquets and people delight in giving them, even to strangers. With a dozen such weapons a tourist can have himself quite a time with the pretty girls along the streets and at the sidewalk cafés. And all lovers feel it a cultural obligation to go off in the neighboring woods to gather their own flowers. This must all be understood to explain the irony the use of the flower has here. In the penultimate line, "les pâles," the bloodless ones, are of course the dead; the poet whose songs once could pierce the marrow of the living must now, being dead himself, sing for his pale countrymen.

Petit mort pour rire, p. 194—

Here we have a plaintive and far-away piping, frail as the soughings of the *mirliton* (reed-pipe) itself. These are songs without words, *chansons sans paroles*, as much as anything ever written. They are elegiac zephyrs blowing over a grave on which grows the *myosotis*, the forget-me-not. And they are the very devil to attempt in rhyme, for here one needs five or six rhymes on one sound. A Petrarchan octave asks only four! These rondels are what Arnoux (pp. 21–22) considers "a naked cry, the twisted heart, the words torn from their natural meaning, in a frenzy which evades both language and grammar." There is something in that line, "Va vite, léger peigneur de comètes," which haunts me, and it is by this phrase— the comet-comber—that I always think of Tristan.

◇   ◇   ◇

While I have worked on these poems, I have grown very close to him, in a way I never could achieve with the loftier Baudelaire—much as I respect him; nor with Verlaine, that song-drunken faun—much as I love him; and especially not with Mallarmé—who intrigues me, but whom I do not love at all. Tristan—I could have gone sailing with him: to me he is very human, and I do not think we shall have much trouble in establishing rapport in Elysium or Limbo.

BIBLIOGRAPHY

EDITIONS OF THE POEMS

Les Amours jaunes (Ça; Les Amours jaunes; Raccrocs; Sérénade des Sé-
rénades; Armor; Gens de mer; Rondels pour après). Paris: Glady
frères, 1873; avec préface de Léon Vanier, Vanier, 1891; édition définitive,
avec préface de Charles Le Goffic, Messein, 1912; avec notice de Réné
Martineau, Crès, 1920; édition définitive, avec préface de Charles Le
Goffic, texte revu par Charles Morice, Messein, 1926; avec une introduc-
tion et des notes de Yves-Gérard Le Dantec, Emile-Paul frères, 1942; avec
préface d'Alexandre Arnoux, Librairie Celtique, 1947; avec préface de
Tristan Tzara, Club Français du Livre, 1950; édition augmentée de poèmes
et proses posthumes, avec introduction et appendice critique par Yves-
Gérard Le Dantec, Gallimard, 1953. [My own work on Corbière was com-
pleted before this 1953 edition by Le Dantec appeared; it is only in my
page proofs that I can include it in this Bibliography.] La Haye: avec
introduction de Jean-Aubry, Stols, 1947.
Armor. Paris: Léon Pichon, 1920; René Helleu, 1936.
Armor et Gens de mer. Le Vésinet (Seine-et-Oise): Dancette, 1946.
Gens de mer. Paris: Vanier, 1891.
La Rapsode foraine et Le Pardon de Sainte-Anne-la-Palud. Paris: Floury,
1920; Crès, 1930.
Litanie du sommeil et autres poëmes ("Voix de la terre": 3; Paris, G.L.M.,
1949). [The "autres poëmes" are "Heures," "Paris," "La Pastorale de
Conlie," "La Fin," "Sonnet posthume," "Rondel," and "Mirliton."]

BOOKS AND ARTICLES

Ajalbert, Jean. *Au temps du symbolisme, 1880–1890* (Paris, Albin Michel,
1938).
——— "En Bretagne: Un poète de la mer," *Figaro,* 31 mai 1890, suppl.
Arréat, Lucien. *Nos poètes et la pensée de leur temps* (Paris, Alcan, 1920).
Arnoux, Alexandre. *Une âme et pas de violon: Tristan Corbière* (Paris,
Grasset, 1930).

Beaufils, Edouard. "Tristan Corbière," *Nouvelle Revue,* 1er septembre 1913.

Bocquet, Léon. *Les Destinées mauvaises* ... (Bibliothèque du Hérisson; Amiens, Edgar Malfère, 1923).

Breton, André. *Anthologie de l'humour noir* (Paris, Editions du Sagittaire, 1950).

Cambry, Jacques. *Voyage dans le Finistère* (3 vols., Paris, 1799), Vol. I.

Carco, Francis. "Corbière, Villon, Verlaine et Rimbaud," *Marches de Provence,* août-septembre 1912.

Chassé, Charles. "Corbière et Baudelaire," *Fureteur Breton,* décembre 1912, janvier 1913.

Clouard, Henri. *La Poésie française moderne, des romantiques à nos jours* (Paris, Gauthier-Villars, 1924).

Davaugour, Simon. *Sous le ciel gris: nouvelles bretonnes* (Paris, Bloud et Cie, 1907).

Durocher, Léon. "Devant Corbière," *Fureteur Breton,* octobre-novembre 1913.

Fontainas, André. *Mes souvenirs du symbolisme* (Paris, Nouvelle Revue Critique, 1928).

Gourmont, Rémy de. *Le Livre des masques* (Paris, Mercure de France, 1896).

Gourvil, Francis. *En Bretagne* ... (Grenoble, Arthaud, 1930).

Huysmans, J.-K. *A rebours* (Paris, Charpentier, 1884).

Johnson, W. Branch. "Death and the Beyond in Breton Folklore," *French Quarterly,* VIII (1936): 32–50.

Kahn, Gustave. "Les Origines du symbolisme, 1879–1888," *La Revue Blanche,* XXVI (1901): 321–348.

———— *Symbolistes et Décadents* (Paris, Vanier, 1902).

———— "Tristan Corbière," *Nouvelle Revue,* XXIX (1904): 271–277.

Laforgue, Jules. *Dragées: Charles Baudelaire, Tristan Corbière* (Paris, La Connaissance, 1921).

———— *Mélanges posthumes* (Vol. III of *Œuvres complètes;* Paris, Mercure de France, 1903).

———— "Notes sur Baudelaire, Corbière, Mallarmé, Rimbaud," *Entretiens Politiques et Littéraires,* II (1891): 20–32.

Le Braz, Anatole. *Aux pays des pardons* (Paris, A. Richard, 1937).

———— *La Légende de la mort chez les bretons armoricains* (5th edition; 2 vols., Paris, Champion, 1928).

Le Goffic, Charles. *Au pays d'Armor* (Paris, E. de Boccard, 1933).

———— *De quelques ombres* (Paris, Lesage, 1930).

——— *Les Poètes de la mer, du moyen âge à nos jours* (Paris, Garnier, 1927).

——— "Tristan Corbière" [same as preface to *Les Amours jaunes*], pp. 163–182 in *L'Ame bretonne* (4ᵉ série; Paris, Champion, 1924).

Levi, Ida. "New Light on Tristan Corbière," *French Studies,* Vol. V, No. 3 (July, 1951), pp. 233–244.

MacIntyre, C. F. Translations of two poems ("Paysage mauvais" and "Petit fort pour rire") in *Envoy: An Irish Review of Literature and Art,* Vol. V, No. 19 (June, 1951), pp. 65–66.

——— "Villon Had a Son: An Essay on Tristan Corbière," *Wake:* 7 (1948), pp. 87 ff.

Marches de Provence, fascicule spécial sur Tristan Corbière, août-septembre 1912.

Martineau, René. "Autour de Tristan Corbière," *Mercure de France,* 16 septembre 1907.

——— *Promenades biographiques* (Paris, Sant' Andrea et Marceron, 1920).

——— *Tristan Corbière* (Paris, Le Divan, 1925).

——— *Types et prototypes* (Paris, Messein, 1931).

——— "Un adversaire de romantisme: Edouard-Antoine Corbière," *Les Annales Romantiques,* II (1905): 325–329.

[Michelet, Emile.] *Portraits du prochain siècle,* I: *Poètes et prosateurs* (Paris, Girard, 1894).

Morice, Charles. "Corbière et Verlaine," *Marches de Provence,* août-septembre 1912.

——— *Tristan Corbière* (Paris, Messein, 1912).

Picard, Gaston. "Tristan Corbière le roscovite," *La Muse Française,* 15 avril 1935.

Quennell, Peter. *Baudelaire and the Symbolists* (London, Chatto & Windus, 1929), pp. 153–178.

Raynaud, Ernest. *La Mêlée symboliste* (Paris, Renaissance du Livre, 1919).

Rousselot, Jean. *Tristan Corbière* ("Poètes d'aujourd'hui": 23; Paris, Editions Pierre Seghers, 1951).

Schuré, Edouard. "Les Légendes de la Bretagne," *Revue des Deux Mondes,* CVI (1891): 408–428.

Souvestre, Emile. *Contes de Bretagne* (Paris, Le Liseron, 1946).

——— *Le Foyer breton* (Paris, Jean Vigneau, 1947).

Thomas, l'abbé J. *Kantikou Santez Anna ar Palud* (Quimper, P. Joncour, 1938).

——— *Sainte Anne la Palud* (Paris, Librairie Celtique, 1946).

Trigon, Jean de. *Tristan Corbière* (Paris, Le Cercle du Livre, 1951).

Van Bever, Ad., et Paul Léautard, *Poètes d'aujourd'hui* (Paris, Mercure de France, 1900).

Verlaine, Paul. *Les Poètes maudits* (Paris, Vanier, 1884).

Visages de la Bretagne [a collection from several authors]. (Paris, Horizons de France, 1941).